THE BEST RUNNING TRAILS
OF THE SAN FRANCISCO BAY AREA

BY BARRY SPITZ, FOREWORD BY WALT STACK

CITY SPORTS PUBLICATIONS
SAN FRANCISCO, CALIFORNIA

Published by City Sports Publications, P.O. Box 3693, San Francisco, California 94119

Type and design by JM Graphics
Photography and cover photo by Lorraine Rorke except as noted
Map illustration by Katherine Tillotson

ISBN 0-932926-01-0
Library of Congress Catalog Card Number 78-73058
Printed in the United States of America
First printing

Contents

Introduction

The best solution to any problem is always the simplest one, and that's why running, so natural and easy to do, has become the ideal way for millions to exercise and stay healthy. I'm a firm believer that running itself should be fun, apart from the physical and mental rewards it brings. And probably the best and surest way to enjoy the sport is to run over different and attractive terrain. That's what this book is all about.

We'll explore trails that will make you glad to be alive, to be outdoors and to be running. The San Francisco Bay Area offers many running courses that are as lovely, quiet and inviting as you'll ever want. This is your guide to 37 such courses.

What makes a great running trail? In this guide, each trail was chosen according to the following standards:

1. A minimum of car traffic. The runs are set in quiet, peaceful surroundings, and many are completely apart from urban distractions of any kind.

2. Attractive scenery. It's hard to go wrong in the Bay Area, but a special point has been made to hit the choicest spots.

3. A comfortable running surface. About half of the runs are on dirt trails, with another half on asphalt, and a few on sand and grass. The surface is described in the heading for each run.

4. An easy-to-follow route. The trails are usually broad and well-marked. Maps accompany each course description.

5. Correct, measured distances. The runs are presented from shortest to longest in length — 1.0 to 8.6

miles. Most of the routes were measured with an AAU-certified measuring wheel, so the distances are accurate. Key mileage markers are noted throughout.

6. Varied terrain. Some of the runs are completely flat, while others have slight grades and easy hills. And for those of you looking for a challenge, there are also a few steep climbs. Based on U.S. Geologic Survey topographical maps, the elevation changes are also given in the run's heading.

7. A loop trail. On each run, you're usually always covering new ground yet you still finish where you start. While a few runs are up-and-back over the same path, only two—the Bay to Breakers and the Bridge to Bridge—don't return you to the starting point.

8. Easy accessibility. Every run is within ten miles of San Francisco Bay (except for one splendid exception, Limantour Spit in Point Reyes). Car directions emanate from San Francisco and public transportation routes are given from the nearest city.

9. No fees. In the spirit of running, you will never have to pay any admission, parking or use fees.

10. Unique attractions besides running. For your entertainment afterwards, or for non-running family or friends, the trails are set in ideal places to have an all-day outing. Many have a special historic or local interest.

But always, the main point is to enjoy yourself. And with the many alternative routes offered, every run affords the possibility of enjoyment again and again.

Finally, I'd like to thank a few people. One is my ever-skeptical typist, Carol Mastick, now a novice runner. Kathy Tillotson, the illustrator, who was a pleasure to work with in drafting the maps. Denise Tong, Johanna Hughes and Margot Meisinger patiently listened to my travails over the many months it took to write this book, and were occasionally asked to push the measuring wheel. And a special tribute to everyone out there pounding the pavement—the plodders, the middle-of-the-packers, the champions—because you've made running the beautiful thing that it is.

Come, let's run.

— *Barry Spitz*

Foreword

Visiting runners to San Francisco and the Bay Area are always asking me where the best places to run are. But my problem is, I never know the directions or anything like that. Barry Spitz has done a real service to residents and visiting runners (and me) by pointing out many of the beautiful running trails here.

Many of these runs—such as San Bruno Mountain in Daly City, the Legion of Honor, Land's End, Baker Beach, Mountain Lake and the Bay to Breakers Practice Run—have been used by the San Francisco Dolphin-South End Runners for the past 13 years. As president and founder of the DSE, and with considerable experience on these trails, I think this book can be a real guide to helping you enjoy running more.

After all, romping amidst this scenery is a treat you deserve. But just because I run back and forth every day across the Golden Gate Bridge from Aquatic Park in San Francisco to Sausalito—that doesn't mean I'm not using these beautiful trails. They are reserved by me for Saturday, Sunday and holidays. Hear that?

Yours in the long run,
Walt Stack

SAN FRANCISCO

Baker Beach

Distance: *1.3 miles*
Hills: *None, level*
Surface: *Sand*

If you think San Francisco lacks beautiful beaches, come to Baker Beach and be surprised. It offers a 2/3 mile stretch of sand, somewhat shielded from the winds by hills on three sides, and framed by some of the loveliest vistas anywhere. And there are usually no more than a handful of people on the beach. So get the leg strengthening benefits of running on sand, and be invigorated.

From the north end of 25th Avenue, take a right onto Lincoln. You're in the Presidio now. Look for the Baker Beach sign on the left, in 1/4 mile. There are parking lots to the left and right; take the right one, where there are bathrooms. The #28 19th Avenue bus (Pershing Drive loop only) goes right by the Baker Beach turnoff. If you've never run without shoes, you might want to try it here. The run is entirely on clean sand. In any case, go down to the water's edge and begin running towards the Golden Gate Bridge.

The sand is, of course, easiest to run on nearest the water, particularly when the tide is going out. Get into your stride, listen to the surf, and soak in the scenery. The beach is named for Colonel Edward Dickinson Baker (as is Fort Baker and Baker Street), who was killed in the Civil War while leading a group of California volunteers. It's 3/8 mile to the rocks. There's another, totally secluded, beach on the other side of the rocks but reach it only at your own peril.

On the return, this view of the neat, colorful houses

of Seacliff, nestled into a cliff at the water's edge, conjures visions of the Riviera. Run past the starting point. The one possible obstacle before the rocks is crossing Lobos Creek, which has its origins at Mountain Lake. If the water's higher than you like, wait a few seconds for it to rush out, or use the creek as another reason to go barefoot.

You'll soon be at the beach's other end. There are steps up to some private residences. Don't take them; just head back to where you started.

Though running on sand is more strenuous than running on other surfaces, you'll still want to do at least one more round trip. That picnic on the beach afterwards will be all the more enjoyable.

Mt. Davidson

Distance: *1.5 miles*
Hills: *275 foot climb, then downhill*
Surface: *Dirt trails, asphalt*

Mt. Davidson, at 938 feet, is the highest point in San Francisco — 16 feet above the taller of the Twin Peaks, and 30 feet higher than Mt. Sutro. It's more noted, however, for the huge concrete cross at its top. It's possible to drive relatively near the summit — the intersection of Myra and Dalewood Ways is closest, just an easy saunter from the top. But the city's highest peak should not be won so easily. Instead, here's a run that is a bit longer and involves a bit more climbing, but still not enough to frighten anyone away.

From Portola Drive, heading southwest, take a left on Evelyn, then a right in two blocks onto Chaves. Park along Chaves. (The #10 Monterey bus is closest, passing along Portola.) Your starting point is the steps leading to Mt. Davidson, between 919 and 925 Rockdale (the continuation of Chaves), near the street's dead end. Remember the address because you may not notice the path otherwise.

Begin by climbing the few steps, then continue on the dirt trail. Already you're in the forest, rich with vegetation. In 175 yards, you'll reach the first intersection. Note the spot because you'll return here from the left when completing the summit loop. Go right now. There are several more forks and small branching paths ahead. Take the left fork at each major intersection (there are four, including the one with the main road). Don't worry; you won't get lost. Just avoid any path narrower than the five-foot one you started with.

In ⅓ mile, you'll reach the main path to the summit. Continue climbing uphill. Look closely for the cross, hidden amidst the tall eucalyptus trees. There are several shortcuts to the top; stick to the main trail because victory is near. Suddenly the crest, and a magnificent vista of the whole expanse of San Francisco Bay, comes into view. You've gained 275 feet in altitude in 2500 feet of running. The cross, 103 feet tall, is right behind you. This is the site of the famous Easter sunrise service.

Catch your breath. Then retrace your steps away from the cross. To the left of the vista point is a short but steep path down to the next level. Go down it slowly. You'll pick up (on the right) the dirt trail that skirts the hill's edge. Enjoy the tremendous view, but also watch your footing as you pick up speed downhill. In just over 300 yards, you'll leave the park at the gate by the intersection of Myra, Dalewood, and Lansdale Streets.

Go left on Myra Way, a very pleasant residential street. It's almost entirely downhill, so you can fly here.

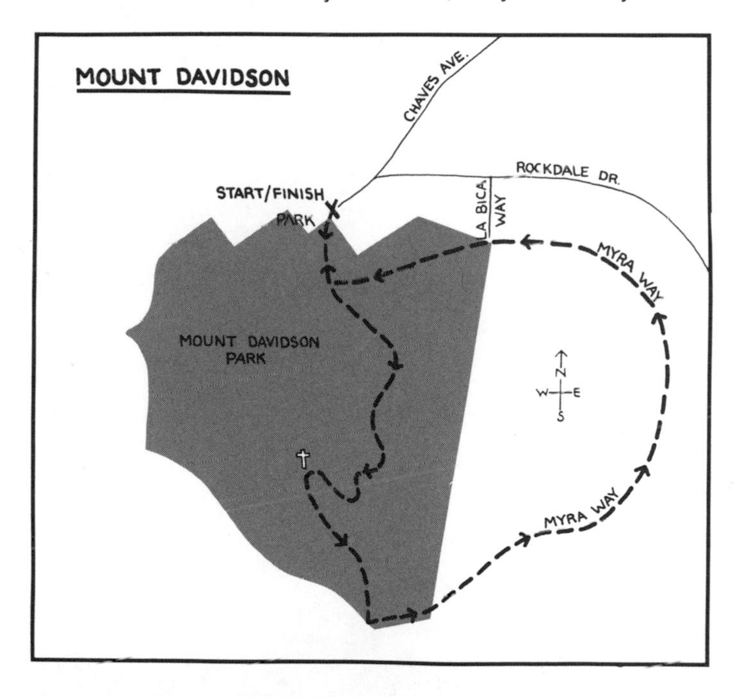

Follow Myra ⅓ mile to its end, at La Bica. You'll see a dirt path entering the park. A different, wider path begins just below. Take either; they join in 200 feet. You should be familiar with the next intersection.Take the downhill fork on the right and retrace the 175 yards to Rockdale.

And now you've climbed the highest point in San Francisco!

Stern Grove

Distance: *2.0 miles*
Hills: *Downhill, level, then 200-ft. climb*
Surface: *Mostly asphalt*

Stern Grove offers much more than the famous free summer Sunday concert series. Come at another time and enjoy, in relative solitude, its steep hills, pleasant meadows, and even a natural lake. This loop course touches four different parks in the area, and finishes right through the heart of the Grove.

Going south on 19th Avenue, take a right on Wawona and park along the street. The #28 bus stops on the corner, as does the #18 Sloat bus one block south. Sigmund Stern Grove is on your left and the Larsen Park swimming pool is on your right. Start here, at 20th and Wawona, and afterwards you can take a shower or swim in the pool. The fee is minimal, but you have to bring your own suit and towel. Also, there are barbecue pits and picnic tables in the Grove.

Begin running down Wawona, a quiet, broad street. In just over ⅓ mile of downhill running, you'll reach the end of the paved road. Wawona continues as a dirt path for two blocks. Run straight. Parkside Square, with baseball fields and tennis courts, is directly uphill. The attractive brick house on your right at 30th is Pinehurst Lodge, a treatment center for female alcoholics. You'll pass a small playground on the left. Enter the park, finally, at 34th Street.

This is actually Pine Lake Park, adjacent to Stern Grove. It's a short downhill to a lake, Laguna Puerca or Pine Lake. Run along the water's left margin. Halfway along is our midway point — one mile. In fall and winter, ducks abound on the lake, and in spring, you'll hear the rowdy frogs in the reeds. At the end of the lake, veer right around a refreshment stand and take a long, paved path to the right of the meadow.

This is a delightful stretch, with tall eucalyptuses crowding out the snarl of traffic. You'll pass a white gate and enter the main Stern Grove parking lot. At the far right end of the lot, the path continues again. Beyond the second white gate is the concert area. As the path runs right behind the stage, feel free to stop and ham it up a bit. Past a third white gate is the old Trocadero Inn. Continue on the main path. Now at last, all that downhill must be repaid.

You've a good stiff climb of some 120 feet in a 1000-foot stretch. But to ease the strain, the trees are tall and dense enough to invoke visions of Sherwood Forest. Soon enough is the main Grove auto entrance, and a rude awakening from your pastoral reveries. Take a left onto the path that parallels busy 19th Avenue. To run exactly 2 miles, follow the paved path to the left when it meets a dirt path leading straight into Wawona. You'll exit Stern Grove at 21st, with the cool, inviting pool to your right.

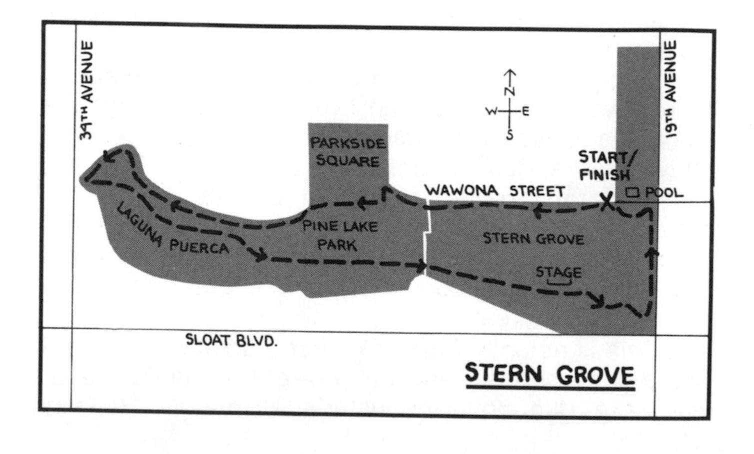

Fort Funston

Distance: *2.3 miles*
Hills: *Half level, 130-ft. climb, then downhill*
Surface: *80% on sand*

The city's southwest corner, anchored by Fort Funston and now almost all part of the Golden Gate National Recreation Area, is among the most magnificent of running areas. This loop follows first the ocean's edge, then returns on cliffs and dunes that afford extraordinary views of the skyline and the Pacific. Just as enticing is the solitude. You are completely apart from cars, from the city's noises, and sometimes even from other people.

Go south on the Great Highway .7 miles past Sloat Boulevard. Park in the last lot by the beach, where the road veers left to join Skyline Boulevard. The parking lot is the run's starting point. Three Muni lines pass nearby: L Taraval, 18 Sloat, and 70 Lake Merced.

Begin running south down the easy path to the water's edge. This is Sand Dollar Beach, named after the sea urchins which are found here. But the tall sand cliffs and the rough surf are the main attractions. Look for the artwork carved on the cliff walls and, in the spring, for nesting bank swallows. When conditions are right, colorful hang gliders soar above. Fort Funston is the most popular, and perhaps only, place to hang glide in the city.

Just short of the one-mile mark, you'll see the masonry for a sewer line outlet. (There have been problems here, making dry passage sometimes difficult.) Immediately, the cliffs fall away from the beach. And in less than ¼ mile, you'll see the first cypress trees at the beach's edge. This is the turning point. Below the Olympic

Club's Ocean Golf Course, the broadest path northward is easy to spot. Start climbing. It gets steep near the summit.

You may be greeted at the top of the path by a flurry of hang gliders waiting their turn to fly. Pass in front of the main Fort Funston parking lot. The fort, established in 1898, was renamed in 1917 for Major General Frederick Funston, commander of the Army troops who maintained order in San Francisco after the 1906 earthquake. You'll see a new, wide trail at the cliff's edge.

In 200 yards or so, a path forks right around the gun batteries. You have magnificent city views as you continue straight. And at your feet are enormous numbers of wild strawberries. As you pass the second bunker, the path slants down to join an asphalt road.

Continue on that road, a beautiful, slightly downhill running surface. You can really get some speed up over this ¼ mile stretch. When the asphalt ends, you face

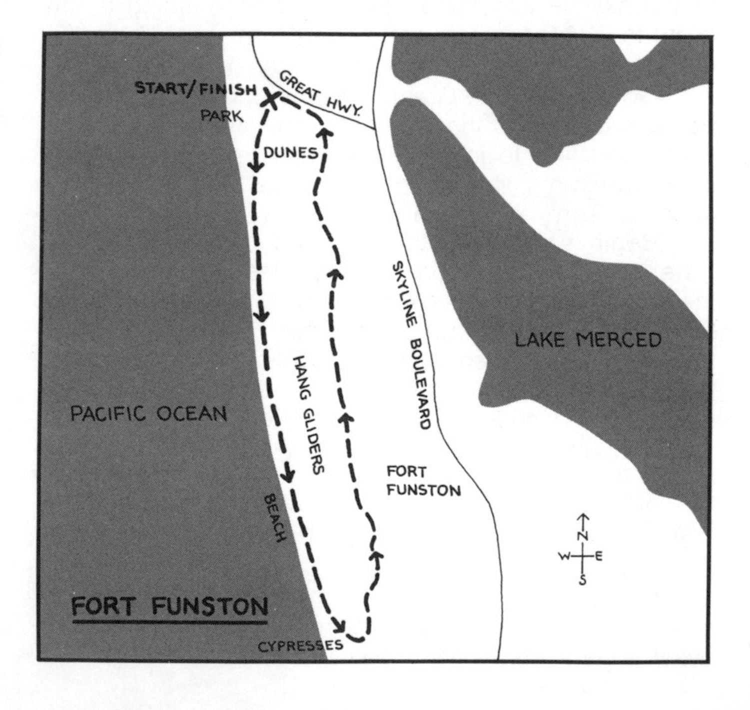

three paths. Take the middle one, going straight over the sand dune and a little bit beyond.

Suddenly, as you hear cars for the first time since you began, the path ends. If you strike off on your own in roughly the same northerly direction, you'll certainly return to the start — though you may have to slide a few feet down a sand bank to do it. The easiest and safest way is to veer toward the highway. You'll join a path that skirts the road. It will lead you through some cypress trees to the parking lot.

If you've still got some energy, just look ahead. The beach stretches invitingly for four more uninterrrupted miles to the Cliff House.

Stow Lake

Distance: *2.44 miles*
Hills: *One 120-ft. climb, otherwise level*
Surface: *Half asphalt, half dirt trails*

Runners are intuitively drawn to the best courses. So there are lots of runners at Stow Lake, for very good reasons. The lake is nestled in the heart of Golden Gate Park, the city's richest running area. It is away from the main roads, and is also the largest of the park's lakes. Stow is circled by a fine running path just longer than one mile. There's an island in the middle — Strawberry Hill — which is remote even by park standards. And there's a special ambiance at Stow Lake, partly due to the many boaters, that makes this a nice place to be and to run. The course will loop first the lake, then the island, then climb to the top of the hill and back.

From Kennedy Drive in the park, take a left at the Stow Lake turnoff, about ½ mile west of the DeYoung Museum. You'll see the boathouse at the top of the short hill. Veer left before you reach it. In less than 300 yards, look for a bridge to the inner island and park along the road by it. This is the starting point. By bus, use the #10 Monterey, which stops at the DeYoung. Also nearby are the #71 Haight-Noriega and the #72 Haight-Sunset on Lincoln Way (on the park's southern side) and the #5 Fulton on the northern border.

Begin running clockwise, to the left when facing the lake. The footpath is easy to run on, and free from bicycles. On the lake you'll see boaters and lots of ducks eager to be fed. One hundred yards past the half-mile mark is the other bridge to the island; don't

Circling Stow Lake

confuse it with the first one! Keep circling the lake. You'll go in front of the boathouse and soon be back at the starting point.

Now cross the bridge to forested Strawberry Hill. You'll see a broad dirt trail, once used by horsedrawn carriages, as soon as you reach the island. Go right, counterclockwise. In 120 yards, there will be a fork. Note it, for you return to this spot. For now, go right, down to the lake's edge. It's quite peaceful on the island and on this little–used path. You'll have a whole different perspective of the lake and the boaters. They'll probably be wondering how you got there. Keep on this lake-level path. It's 400 yards to the second bridge and 900 yards for the full loop.

Continue around again to the fork. This time, go left, and get ready for some climbing. This is one of the most isolated parts of the entire park. Just keep chugging, as the vistas keep broadening. In ¼ mile, you reach the first crest, by a reservoir. 300 yards farther is a second crest, the highest point we reach on the run. Strawberry Hill's 412-foot summit is just to the left. The views here are superb, with an unmatched 360-degree panorama. You've climbed 120 feet in 2,250 feet of running. You end up taking the same path down, though the loop near the top may make you think otherwise. It's the only trail

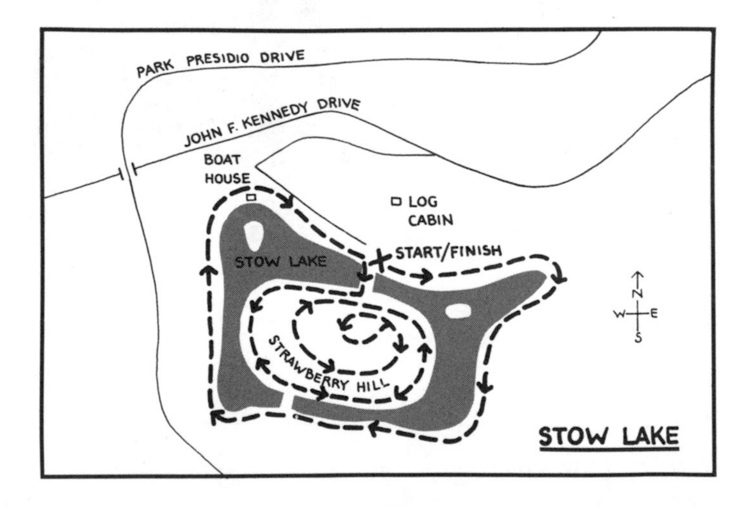

on the hill, apart from some very steep and narrow ones.

Keep straight when you return to the island loop trail and you'll be at the bridge across from your car in 120 yards. Now how about circling the lake still a different way, on the water.

Golden Gate Park 5 Kilometer Loop

Distance: *3.1 miles (5 kilometers)*
Hills: *One of 50 ft., otherwise gently rolling*
Surface: *Asphalt and dirt*

There's a loop course in Golden Gate Park that is almost precisely five kilometers — just four or so meters short. It is the site of many races, occasionally even of a national Amateur Athletic Association (AAU) Championship. The loop is in the quieter western half of the park. It also encounters only two cross streets in its entire length. So while you're becoming familiar with a course you may one day be racing on, you're enjoying a pleasant run as well.

Park in the lot at the western end of the Polo Fields, off Middle Drive. This is the usual starting point for races, so you'll use it, too. By bus, take either the #72 Haight-Sunset on Lincoln or the #5 Fulton, get off near 36th Avenue, and take the short walk to the Polo Fields. There are bathrooms and a fountain by the Polo Fields' southern entrance.

Begin running east on Middle Drive, keeping the Polo Fields on your left. There's a gentle upslope, as is often the case going east in Golden Gate Park. You'll pass Metson Lake, on the right. In one kilometer, the road forks. Veer left onto Overlook Drive. The upgrade is more noticeable here. At the end of this road go left, then quickly take another left onto Kennedy Drive.

This is the Park's main thoroughfare. But if you run on the path to the left, which is first asphalt then dirt, the

Rounding a turn on race day

cars won't be bothersome. This long downslope is a good chance to stretch your legs. The one–mile mark is at the first of several meadows you pass on the left. Lindley Meadow is perhaps the loveliest and is also famous for its totem pole.

You'll catch only glimpses of the landmarks on the right — Lloyd Lake, Marx Meadow, then Spreckels Lake. Continue straight on the gently downhill path as Kennedy Drive briefly splits at aptly–named Rhododendron Island. The buffalo enclosure quickly appears on your right. Soon, to the left, is the entrance to the Anglers' Lodge.

The first intersection, with Chain of Lakes Drive, is the two–mile mark. This is a four-way stop for cars. You're also near the Bercut Equitation Field, to the left, so watch your step. The ocean, as you'll notice, is increasingly felt in the vegetation and in the air.

The path will end at a crossroad, just beyond the nine-hole Municipal Golf Course. Loop to the left. You're on South Drive now, heading east. A parallel path begins on the left. You'll soon run into the only other cross street, Chain of Lakes Drive (again). South Lake, the smallest of the three Chain of Lakes, is just to the left. This is the home stretch if you're only going around once, so start picking up momentum.

At the next fork, with Middle Drive, go left. Though most course descriptions say otherwise, this is a hill, albeit a short one. It's ⅕ mile long and you gain around

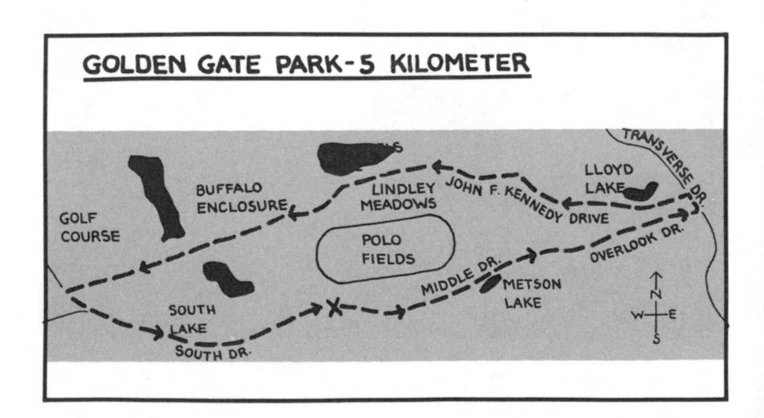

50 feet. At the top, you're back at the starting line.

Check your watch and try another loop. The course record for five loops, or 25 kilometers, is one hour, seventeen minutes, and twenty-two seconds, by Jim Nuccio.

Mountain Lake — Presidio Heights

Distance: *3.29 miles*
Hills: *One of 150 ft.; one of 105 ft.*
Surface: *Mostly asphalt*

This is a particularly charming run. You go out on a pastoral trail just inside the Presidio's south wall and return through Presidio Heights, with its majestic mansions. There are two modest hills to contend with. You climb them in the first half to enjoy a predominantly downhill run back.

The starting point is at an entrance to Mountain Lake Park, a few yards north of Lake Street on 9th Avenue. The park is easy to miss — it's well hidden and there are no signs. Park along Lake, or in the several culs-de-sac just north of it. The #1 California, the #2 Clement, and the #38 Geary buses all pass within three blocks south of Lake.

Begin running to the left (west) on the path just inside the park. This is also the beginning of a Parcourse that loops the park. You'll pass ball fields and tennis courts. The trail then veers right, by bathrooms and a fountain. Continue to the right when you reach Mountain Lake. This is one of the city's few natural lakes and it retains a pristine appearance despite the nearby highway.

Just past the lake is a fork. Leave the park by veering to the left of the stone Presidio wall, onto a dirt trail. This quickly joins a long, straight, traffic-free road, West Pacific Avenue. Continue on it in your same easterly direction. Going left is tempting — it will lead you around

Mountain Lake and Parcourse

the lake, under the freeway, through a gate, and out by the Public Health Service Hospital. But save that for another time; this run is nicer.

Begin climbing the first hill. There's pleasant scenery and the path is well-shaded. You gain 150 feet in 2250 feet of running. By the crest is the Presidio Golf Course Clubhouse. In less than 200 yards, you'll reach the Arguello Gate to the Presidio. Keep on the same path, just to the left of the wall.

As you begin the downhill, you pass the run's one–mile mark. There's a parallel dirt trail to the left, along the forest's edge. Or stay on the road for better views of Presidio Heights, among the most exclusive parts of San Francisco. At the bottom of the hill is Julius Kahn Playground.

Now for the second hill. It's about as steep as the first, but shorter. Keep on the paved road. As you hear and see Presidio Boulevard just ahead, a dirt trail crosses the road. This is straight, tree-lined Lover's Lane. Take it uphill to the right. (Try the Presidio Loop run for a longer stay on it.) You'll soon be at the Presidio Gate, and the hill's summit.

If you don't want anything to do with city streets, however peaceful and lovely, return over the same route. This round trip also measures almost exactly 3.29 miles.

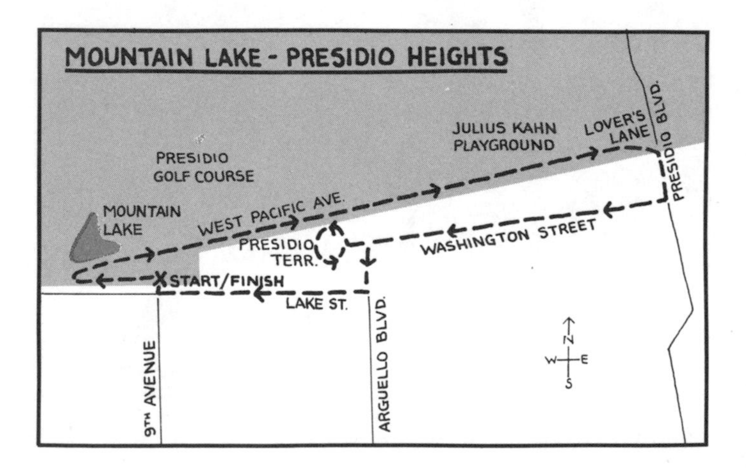

Continue by running two blocks south on Presidio Avenue, then going right onto Washington. For the next mile, you'll pass scores of stately single family residences. And at the generally empty intersections are terrific views, north and south. A few yards short of Laurel Street is the run's two–mile point.

Washington Street ends at Arguello, directly in front of Presidio Terrace. Enter through the gate and run right, around the loop. Back on Arguello, turn right in front of domed Temple Emanu-El. Take another right when you reach Lake Street.

There's traffic along Lake, but also a bike path. The three–mile mark is midway between 4th and 5th Avenues, shortly beyond the main entrance to St. Anne's Hospital. Open up and sprint home to 9th Avenue.

The Golden Gate Bridge

Distance: *3.4 miles*
Hills: *Two gentle rises*
Surface: *Cement*

Running across the Golden Gate Bridge is, despite the cars, a fantastic experience. There just may be no more exciting or scenic course anywhere. By concentrating on the running, on the bridge itself, and on the great views, you can learn to almost shut out the noise. Give it a try.

Stay in the right lane as you approach the bridge on Highway 101. Take the last exit, just in front of the toll booths. The viewing area and parking lot is immediately to the left. Or avoid Doyle Drive and reach the same spot from the Presidio's Lincoln Boulevard, approaching from either direction. The #28 19th Avenue bus stops at the toll plaza. There are public restrooms in the Roundhouse, which is also used for Bridge District offices. Dress warmly, because the winds may be blustery.

The pedestrian path to the bridge from the parking lot is well-marked. You'll see where the trail from the Golden Gate Promenade and Fort Point terminates. You'll also see the bike path that leads under the bridge to the west side. It's worth taking this short stretch for a unique view. The gate onto the bridge's west side is closed except on weekends, when only bicyclists can use it.

Begin the run on the right sidewalk at the south end of the bridge. The gate is open from six a.m. to nine p.m. and you're no longer expected to drop ten cents into a turnstile, a tradition that was honored more in the breach than in the observance.

Crossing the Golden Gate

For once, you can't possibly lose the path. And the scenery needs hardly be described. It's stunning, period. Get into your stride and savor the moment. You may be alone on the bridge, or there may be strollers, bicyclists, and other runners. Why not say hello? You're all sharing something special.

The whole bridge is 8,981 feet long. It is 4,200 feet between the towers and 6,450 feet between the massive concrete pylons. The towers are 746 feet tall. Note the different surface as you go around them, as sliding joints compensate for expansion and contraction. There's a gentle uphill to the point where the great supporting cables reach the bottom of their arc. Here you are 220 feet above the high water mark and at one of the most famous spots on earth.

Continue on to the end of the bridge, at the entrance to the northern viewing area. There's a convenient water fountain. Also here is the path emerging from the west side.

Run back, perhaps joining another runner. And say hello again to the walkers you passed on the way out.

Presidio Loop

Distance: *4.6 miles*
Hills: *Rolling, one gradual 250-ft. climb*
Surface: *Mostly asphalt, some dirt trails*

Sooner or later, everyone who runs in San Francisco is drawn to the Presidio. Here, on some 1500 acres in the city's northwest, are thick forests, hills commanding magnificent vistas, historic buildings, and hidden trails. It is a military installation, to be sure, headquarters for the Sixth Army. But the hiker and runner are completely welcome.

The course loops past many of the Presidio's finest features. Use either the Presidio Avenue or Lombard Street entrance. Just past where these two streets join, veer left, staying on Presidio. Take the second left, Barnard Avenue, and park here. The #28 19th Avenue bus, Chestnut and Fillmore branch only, passes within one block of the starting point. Get off at Funston and Presidio and go up Funston to Moraga Avenue.

Begin by running up the steps where Fernandez, the first intersecting street, ends at Barnard. This puts you onto Moraga. Run straight past the Officer's Club and the old comandante's headquarters, whose sign proclaims it to be the oldest building in San Francisco. The vast parade grounds are to the right. Past the Presidio Playhouse and Theatre, Moraga dead ends at Infantry Terrace. Go right, downhill, passing the Post Chapel and Music Center. You'll catch sight of the Golden Gate Bridge. Head towards it by veering left on Sheridan. Keep left as you join busy Lincoln Boulevard by the main entrance to the National Military Cemetery.

This is the run's noisiest section — after all, Doyle

The stillness of the Presidio

Drive is below you. Continue on Lincoln around the cemetery's wall, bypassing the road leading to Crissy Field. You are beginning the run's major uphill section. At the next big intersection, with McDowell, leave Lincoln (and the 49–Mile Drive) by going left onto Park Boulevard. Continue until you see the stone gate entrance to Fort Winfield Scott. Enter it, right under Highway 1. This is also the run's one–mile mark.

You're on Kobbe Avenue now. Keep chugging uphill, past the large, majestic homes. It's more peaceful

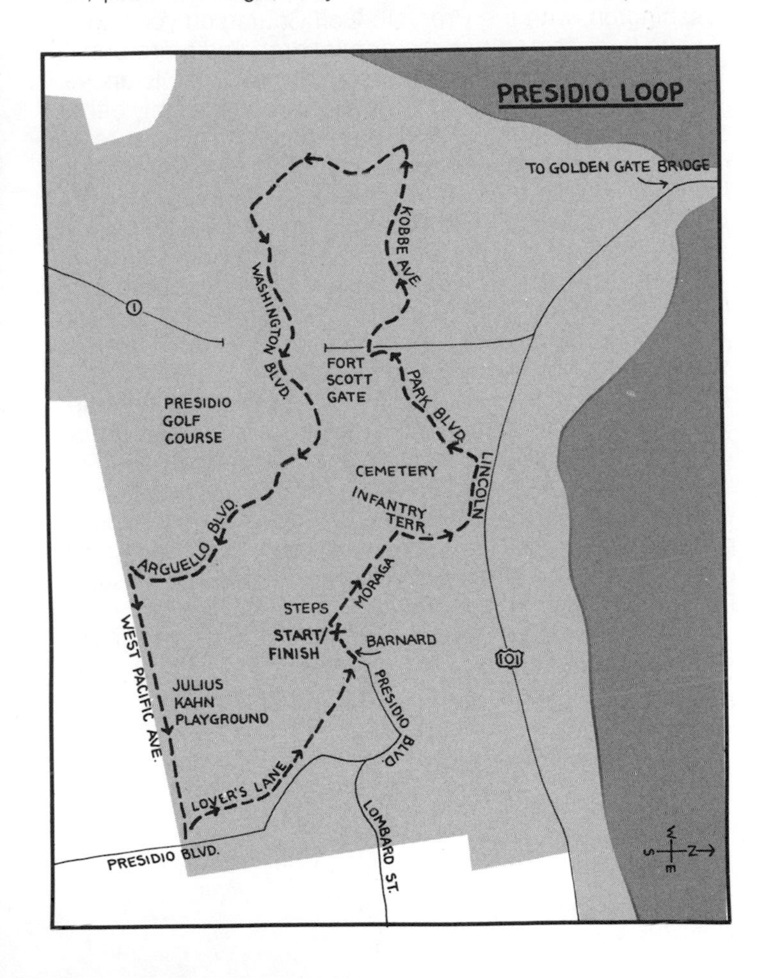

and remote here. A half-mile from where you entered the Fort, you will come to the intersection with Washington Boulevard. Go left on it. The impressive West Coast Memorial is right below you.

Now a reward for your uphill efforts (though there is still some climbing ahead): the views are stunning. You are higher than Lincoln Boulevard, where cars heading to and from the Golden Gate Bridge pull into lookout points. You'll soon enter a post residential area, in the middle of which is the run's two–mile point. Keep on Washington, with the Presidio Golf Course on your right. You go through another residential area and more uphill. The Presidio's highest point, just under 400 feet, is above.

Washington ends at Arguello. Proceed right, either on the road or on the dirt path beside it. Be sure to glance to the left as you pass the Inspiration Point parking area. This is the run's three–mile mark. Just before reaching the Arguello gate out of the Presidio, take a left onto West Pacific Avenue, with the wall to your right.

This stretch is covered in the Mountain Lake run. It's quite popular with runners. A dirt path follows the paved road. Enjoy the mansions of Presidio Heights. You'll soon go by Julius Kahn Playground.

In another ⅓ mile, within sight of Presidio Avenue, you will see a long, straight, tree-lined downhill path on your left. It's really unmistakable for it is one of the loveliest, most inviting stretches in the city. The path is called Lover's Lane. Stretch your legs now for a completely glorious half-mile. Picture yourself in a bygone era — as this is the route of the old Spanish Mission Dolores-Presidio trail — and fly.

You'll cross MacArthur Street. The path continues straight ahead across a bridge over El Polin Creek. And you're back at Barnard. Run left towards your car.

Lake Merced

Distance: *5.0 miles*
Hills: *None, very gentle rolls*
Surface: *Asphalt and dirt*

What a superb loop course Lake Merced offers — five uninterrupted miles around the city's largest lake. There are always lots of runners circling the lake's shores, which makes for a good atmosphere. But the trail is long and broad enough to give everybody elbow room. Indeed, on a race day, 1000 runners may be accommodated.

Join Skyline Boulevard at its beginning, the junction of Sloat and Sunset Boulevards in the city's southwest corner. Follow Skyline, Highway 35, ¾ mile and take a left at the big wooden sign for Lake Merced-Harding Park. The #70 Lake Merced bus stops here. The sign also says "Golf Course, Driving Range, Fishing, Boating, Restaurants, Picnic Areas, Sailing." Add "Running" and you've now got lots of reasons to come with a friend and make this an all-day outing.

Drive past the boathouse, which has bathrooms, water fountains, and places to eat. Beyond is an open gate and parking areas to the left and right. Dolphin-South End Running Club races begin here. It is also where the mileage markers on the trail are measured from. By beginning here, and finishing a few yards beyond, this is a five-mile run. Circling the lake itself is only 4.44 miles. You might want to time yourself. The markers, found every half-mile around the lake, are accurate.

Begin running back towards the entrance. When

you reach Skyline Boulevard, go right, clockwise around the lake. Run on the asphalt path, or on the parallel dirt trail that continues on and off over the entire loop. To the left is the Recreation Center for the Handicapped. You'll soon notice the first of the mileage markers, a "½" painted on the path's right edge. Next is the San Francisco Zoo, still another choice for activities after the run. Lake Merced Boulevard replaces Skyline as the border road. The one–mile mark is at the southern end of Sunset Boulevard, an alternative starting point for those taking the #72 Haight-Sunset bus. Most runners continue directly on the circular loop, rather than following the path's curve around the parking lots.

There's a pleasant residential district on your left, followed by Lowell High School. Past Winston Drive is the San Francisco State University campus. You'll leave the lake for a shaded stretch with Harding Park Golf Course on the right. The two–mile mark is here, just

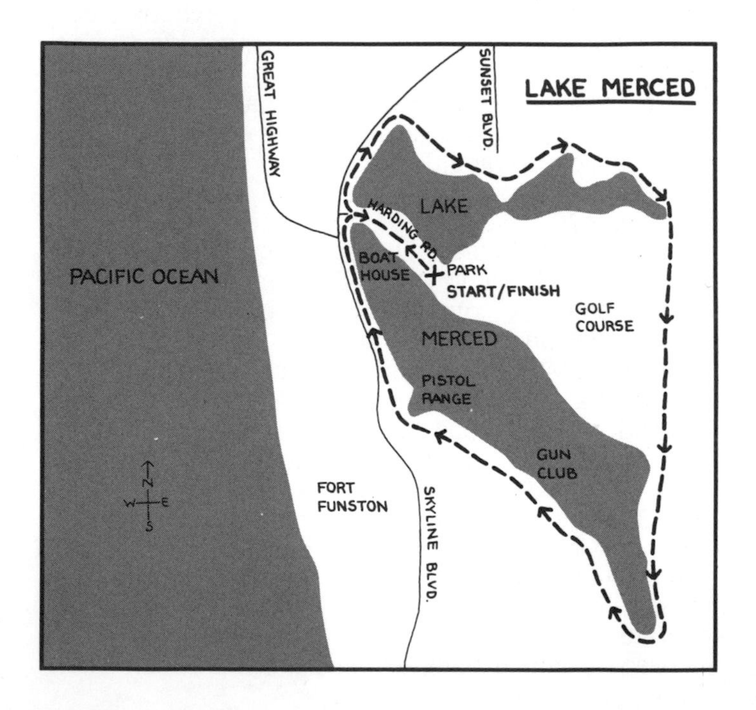

before the first Park Merced tower. The course slopes gently downward as you rejoin the lake near Brotherhood Way. Enjoy! The lake was once an ocean lagoon until sand dunes cut it off from the sea. It is now fresh water, fed by underground streams.

The path turns, a few yards short of the three-mile mark, around the lake's southern tip. You're at the San Mateo County line. Continue around the lake; the adjacent street is John Muir Boulevard. The Olympic Country Club's Lakeside Golf Course is to the left. You'll feel the gradual slope here, the closest to a hill on the course. The gunshots you hear are from The Pacific Rod and Gun Club.

The four–mile mark is just before the intersection with Skyline and the green fence that surrounds the San Francisco Police pistol range. Keep pulling, you're almost home. You'll see the Great Highway's terminus. Turn right at the Lake Merced-Harding Park sign. Open up — it's 500 yards to the finish. Go 55 yards beyond the starting line, to the first painted bump in the road, and you've run exactly 5 miles.

Land's End — Legion of Honor

Distance: *6.1 miles*
Hills: *One of 220 feet, one of 210 feet*
Surface: *Dirt and asphalt*

There are only a handful of areas in San Francisco where you can completely escape from the noises of the city. Land's End is one such area. Here the sounds are of seals and wind through cypresses and pounding surf. And the views are of the Marin headlands and the Golden Gate. Your run begins at Land's End, continues through the Sea Cliff district, scales a hill in the Presidio that affords stunning vistas, then returns past the Palace of the Legion of Honor.

To reach the start, go west on Geary Boulevard. Continue on its branch, Point Lobos Avenue. Past 48th Ave., opposite Sutro Heights Park, turn right into Merrie Way and park. The #2 Clement ends its run just uphill at 48th. Your trail begins at the lot's north end. There's a Golden Gate National Recreation Area sign to mark it; unfortunately, it proclaims "No Dumping" rather than "Welcome."

Begin running on the dirt path through the shade of the cypresses, while the seals yelp on the rocks below. In just over 100 yards, at the first major fork, keep on the broad path by veering right and upward. In 100 feet, you join the main trail. Take it left.

The path is fairly level and well-maintained. You'll soon get your first glimpse of the Golden Gate Bridge. Just above you is the monument to those who went down with the U.S.S. San Francisco at the Battle of Guadalcanal. The intersecting paths on the right climb toward the Veteran's Hospital. Those to the left descend to the rocks below, but the footing is treacherous. It's lovely enough just where you are, so keep on the main trail.

Just under ¾ miles into the run, the path encounters a short, rocky section. Clamber over the remains of steps, then keep running in the same direction towards Baker Beach. At the one-mile mark, you cross wooden planks that bridge a sometimes muddy stretch. It is 300 yards more to the path's end, at the junction with El Camino del Mar.

You can turn here and run back on the same path to make a traffic-free 2.7 mile run. But for this run, continue by veering left. The park quickly gives way to the lovely mansions of the Sea Cliff district. El Camino splits into an upper and lower road. Take either path because they rejoin. The left onto Seacliff Avenue, which leads to James Phelan State Beach, is tempting. But save it for another day and continue on El Camino del Mar.

There's a major intersection at 25th Ave. Continue straight; you're on Lincoln Boulevard. A sign welcomes you to the Presidio. The Baker Beach turnoff is next, on your left. And now, get ready to climb.

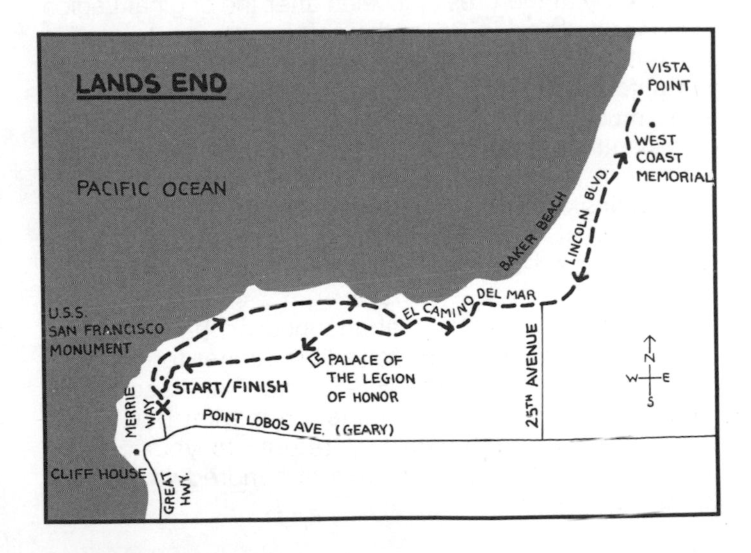

The 210-foot uphill begins gradually. It picks up in earnest after the last of the residential area to the right. Just take it nice and easy, walk if you must. The scenery is magnificent. Stick to the left margin, as far as possible from the drivers who may be looking at the vistas and not at the road.

When you spot the sign for the World War II monument, you know you've made it. The crest, at 280 feet, is just beyond, at the junction with Washington Boulevard. There's a lookout here and this view is to be found in photo albums across the world. You can reach the Golden Gate Bridge by continuing on Lincoln for about ½ mile, then taking a left just beyond the freeway overpass to reach the sidewalk of the bridge's east side. But running beyond this point, unless you cross the bridge, is anti-climactic.

Retrace your steps down that glorious downhill. It seems shorter this way, doesn't it? Then it's back, on a gentle upslope, through Sea Cliff. The second major uphill, 220 feet over ½ mile, begins as you re-enter Lincoln Park. You'll pass the trail from Land's End, and continue climbing up El Camino del Mar. Your perseverance will be rewarded, as the Palace of the Legion of Honor stands majestically at the crest. Modeled after the original Legion of Honor building in Paris, the palace was completed in 1924. It was a gift of the Spreckels family as a memorial to Californians killed in World War I, and now houses an art museum.

Continue straight on the paved road past the building's north face. The pavement soon ends, and a dirt trail begins. There are a few twists at first, just keep heading west. You're running parallel to and above the path you came out on. So the views are even broader now.

Soon you'll meet an abandoned asphalt roadway. People collect the aromatic, edible fennel found here. It's a straight path to the U.S.S. San Francisco Monument. Just to the monument's left, a marker points to a very short but steep path that returns to your original trail. Veer left. It's only a couple of hundred yards back to the starting point.

Palace of the Legion of Honor

Bay to Breakers

Distance: *7.6 miles*
Hills: *One of 180 feet, another more gradual*
Surface: *Concrete, asphalt*

The Bay to Breakers is the king of all races in the Bay Area. Indeed, it is the second-oldest continuous road race in the world (behind the Boston Marathon) and has led all races in total participants for years. Begun in 1910, the race has introduced thousands of people to long distance running, to racing, to the fraternity of runners. It may be fashionable to criticize the race because of the crowds, but when May rolls around, the fever becomes irresistible. Even though the course is one-way and the first several miles are over less than ideal conditions, it is still a great run.

The course begins at the intersection of Howard and Spear Streets, by the Rincon Annex Post Office. There's metered and lot parking nearby on weekdays. Actually, if you plan on running one–way, you might find it better to park at the other end, along the Great Highway between Fulton and Lincoln. Then take either the #5 Fulton bus from La Playa and Fulton to Market and Spear, or the #38 Geary from Cabrillo and the Great Highway to the East Bay bus terminal. Both buses are convenient at each end. Then you finish by your car and don't have to travel by Muni afterwards. The ideal way to do this run, of course, is to have a friend drop you off at Howard and Spear early one Sunday morning, meet you at the top of the Hayes Street hill with an orange slice, then wait for you with a change of clothes and a cold drink at the finish. Then you buy that good person brunch at the Cliff House.

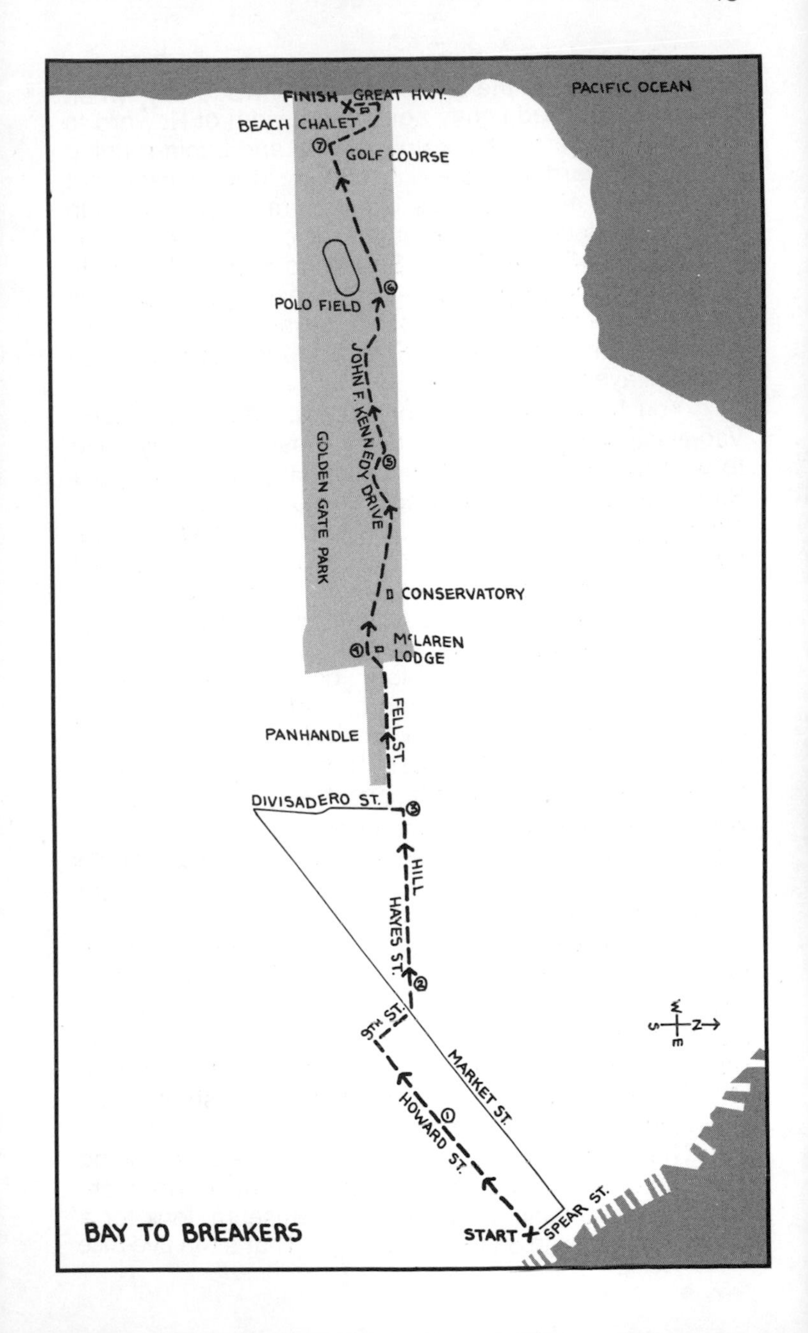
FINISH
GREAT HWY.
PACIFIC OCEAN
BEACH CHALET
GOLF COURSE
POLO FIELD
JOHN F. KENNEDY DRIVE
GOLDEN GATE PARK
CONSERVATORY
McLAREN LODGE
FELL ST.
PANHANDLE
DIVISADERO ST.
HILL
HAYES ST.
9TH ST.
MARKET ST.
HOWARD ST.
SPEAR ST.
START
W
S
N
E
BAY TO BREAKERS

You're at Howard and Spear, ready to run. Go to the northwest corner, the choicest spot on race day, when bodies are packed tightly across the width of Howard to the Embarcadero. Check your watch and begin running west on Howard. It's safe only on the sidewalk except at the quietest of times. This is a commercial area, with small factories and warehouses. The one-mile mark is just past 5th Street. At 9th Street, go right. It's okay to cut through the gas station — countless thousands have done it before you. Keep on the left side of 9th for two blocks, then cross Market Street. Go left at the beginning of Hayes Street.

You have a long run on Hayes. When you reach Van Ness, you've gone two miles. Again, you may have to wait to cross here. Continue on Hayes past Laguna Street, which marks the beginning of the famous five-block long Hayes Street Hill. You'll gain 180 feet in elevation over 2350 feet of running, a good–sized hill. But just envision all the moaning and groaning on race day, and chug to the crest. Alamo Square is to the right, the Louise Lombard School on the left.

There's now a two–block downhill. Just before Divisadero, another busy intersection to cross, is the run's three-mile point. Take Divisadero left one block, then go right onto Fell Street. That's the last turn until the Great Highway. In two blocks, the grassy Panhandle begins, the gateway to Golden Gate Park. Run in it, if you want, but it's easier on Fell. You'll notice a gentle uphill on this stretch. Then, at last, enter the Park by crossing Stanyan Street.

Take the Park's main road, John F. Kennedy Drive, for its entire length. The road is closed to traffic on Sundays above Cross-Over Drive. The course's four-mile mark is near the start of the park, by McLaren Lodge, the Recreation and Park Department's headquarters. You're at 250 feet elevation here. Except for a few small rises, it's mostly downhill to the ocean.

The Conservatory, with its impressive surrounding floral arrangements, appears on the right. Farther on, after you pass behind the DeYoung Museum, look for a "Rest Room" sign on the road's right.That's the five-mile mark. You'll run by the Rose Garden, the turn for Stow Lake, and Prayerbook Cross before going under the Highway 1 bridge. Now the Park is more peaceful, and the course goes downhill. Run on the dirt trail to the left, the road itself, or on the asphalt path on the right.

The next landmark, on the right, is Lloyd Lake, with its white marble portico called "Portals of the Past." The portals stood in a Nob Hill mansion before the earthquake. There are lovely meadows to the left. Lindley Meadow marks the run's six-mile point. Look for the totem pole, carved from a single tree for the 1939 Golden Gate Exposition. Spreckels Lake, noted for its model yachts, appears to the right. Just beyond, Kennedy Drive splits briefly for Rhododendron Island. Continue and you'll see the buffalo enclosure to the right.

Perhaps the loveliest stretch of all begins past Chain of Lakes Drive. You know victory is near as you taste the salty air. It's downhill and quiet. Kennedy Drive veers right, and we follow it, at the intersection past the Municipal Golf Course. This is the run's seven-mile mark. You can really open up on this last downhill.

And so you reach the Great Highway. Cut left. The explorer Amundsen's ship "Gjoa" stood here for years. Now only his statue remains. Keep along the left edge of the road for about 300 yards. The finish is the fifth light pole beyond the Beach Chalet. (On race day, however, unless you're among the leaders, the backup at the finish line will force you to stop a bit earlier.)

You made it!

Bridge to Bridge

Distance: *7.93 miles*
Hills: *One of 75 feet, otherwise level*
Surface: *Asphalt, cement and some gravel*

San Francisco's northern waterfront houses many of the city's most famous attractions. It also contains several of its best and most popular running trails. This run will cover its full length — from the Ferry Building to Fort Point and back to the Marina Green — along the course of the annual Bridge to Bridge race. But you can choose sections of the route for shorter runs.

If it's possible, a car shuttle is best, since the full round trip is 11 miles. Park your car by the Marina Green at the foot of Fillmore Street. Then take the other car to the Ferry Building, at Embarcadero and Market Street, where you'll have to pay to park. Or use the #30 Stockton bus as transportation between the start and finish. The stop closest to the Marina Green is at Fillmore and Chestnut, while the stop at Sutter and Kearny is closest to the Ferry Building.

To time yourself, look up at the Ferry Building's huge clock, whose 11-foot minute hand and 7-ft. hour hand stopped for almost one year at 5:12 a.m. on April 18, 1906 — the moment of the earthquake. (The Larkspur ferry terminal is housed here, but the boat traffic is a faint echo of pre-Bay Bridge days when the Ferry Building was second only to London's Charing Cross station in the annual number of passengers.) Begin running north, the direction of the odd-numbered piers, along the Embarcadero. You'll see many lunch-time runners beginning here as well. Others head down the Embarcadero in the opposite direction — towards the YMCA and China Basin.

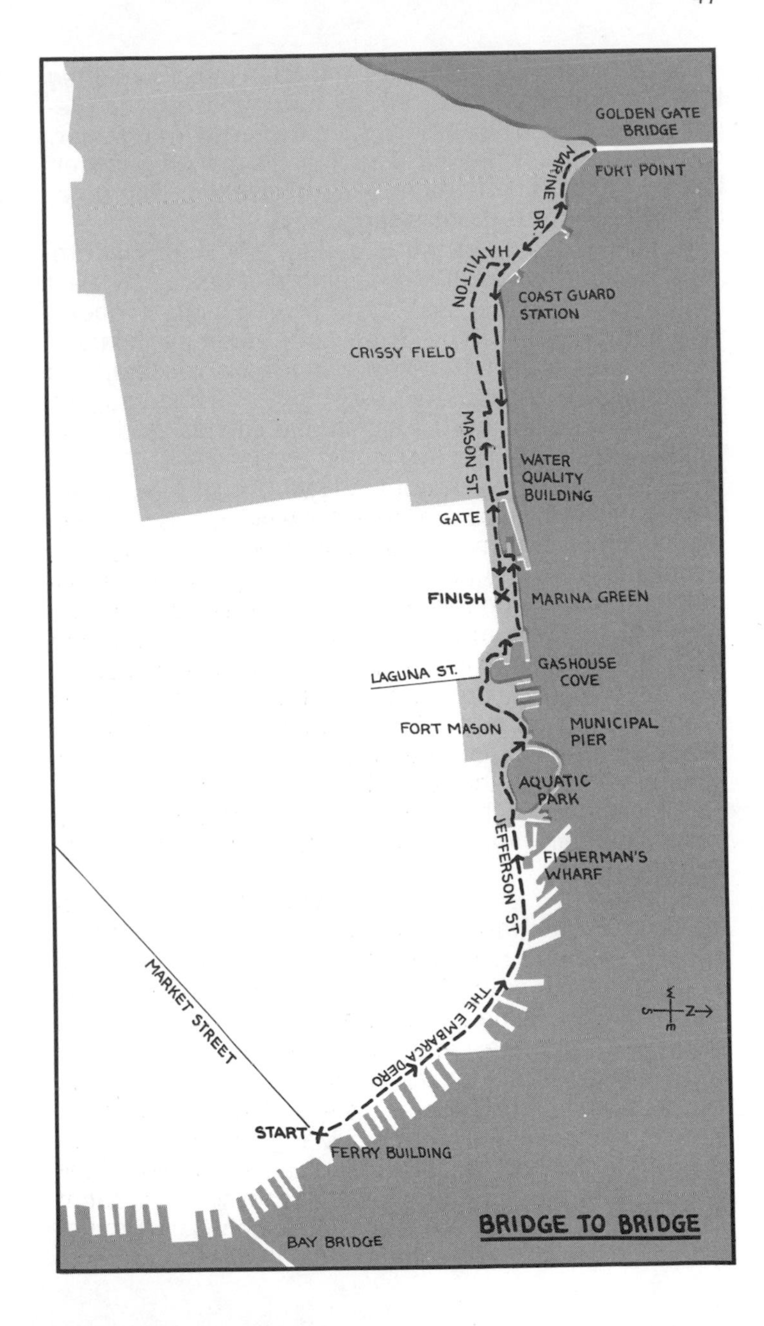
GOLDEN GATE BRIDGE
FORT POINT
MARINE DR.
HAMILTON
COAST GUARD STATION
CRISSY FIELD
MASON ST.
WATER QUALITY BUILDING
GATE
FINISH
MARINA GREEN
LAGUNA ST.
GASHOUSE COVE
FORT MASON
MUNICIPAL PIER
AQUATIC PARK
JEFFERSON ST
FISHERMAN'S WHARF
THE EMBARCADERO
MARKET STREET
START
FERRY BUILDING
BAY BRIDGE
BRIDGE TO BRIDGE
N
S
E
W

You'll pass several piers that have been converted to office buildings. The freeway above goes to its premature death and Telegraph Hill, crowned by Coit Tower, comes into view on the left. The one-mile mark is between Piers 31 and 33. You might see a passenger ship here; otherwise the waterfront is sadly quiet.

Activity picks up at the huge Pier 39 shopping complex, with its scores of restaurants and boutiques. Past the Balclutha, "The Last Cape Horn Square Rigger," veer left onto Jefferson Street and enter the heart of Fisherman's Wharf. There are sidewalk vendors, and lots of people and cars, so expect to do some dodging. Just relax and absorb the sights and sounds. And don't forget, you are at a real live tourist attraction.

Continue straight past the Hyde Street Pier, where several historic ships are open for viewing. To the right are the famed swimming and rowing clubs — the Dolphin, South End, and the defunct San Francisco club. Now, at last, there are no more cars and a clear view of the Bay. You're in Aquatic Park. Look for swimmers in the cove, the run's two-mile mark. On the incline to your left is the city's Maritime Museum, built in 1938 by the W.P.A. Follow the old railroad tracks to the street, the peaceful terminus of Van Ness Avenue. The tracks continue through the tunnel, a level shortcut under Fort Mason. Go right to Black Point and the 1850-foot municipal pier. Veer uphill on the paved road into Fort Mason.

This former Army base is now the headquarters of the Golden Gate National Recreation area. As you tackle the course's one hill, enjoy the views and what is reportedly the last natural vegetation on this shore of San Francisco Bay. At the top is a pleasant, tree-shaded area. Below are the three piers that served as the principal Army docking facility on the Pacific during World War II.

At a huge sign "Piers," veer left for a short way, then immediately go right onto MacArthur Avenue. It's downhill to the Fort Mason exit on Laguna Street, at the Marina Safeway. Run toward the Gashouse Cove Yacht Harbor parking area. You'll spot a Golden Gate Promenade sign — the path that skirts the shore to Fort

Start of the first annual Bridge To Bridge Run

Point. Follow it. At the first left are bathrooms, a fountain, and the start of a popular 18-station Parcourse.

Here begins the fabled Marina Green, with the greatest concentration of runners in the Bay Area. Stay on the asphalt, or join the scores of runners on the well-worn path at the edge of the grassy field. The Green's length is 586 yards and its width — which you cover by going left at the Harbor Master's station — is 60 yards. Continue to the right, beside the West Harbor. Busy Marina Boulevard is on your left and the city's mooring slips for boats is on the right. You then reach the small western area of the Marina Green, popular with sunbathers and volleyballers.

The Bridge to Bridge course continues straight through the Presidio gate. (If the gate is closed, run on the road past the bathrooms on your right to the stone steps of the Water Quality Control building. Continue west on the Promenade at the bay's edge.) Enter the Presidio and run past the old supply buildings along Mason Street. Highway 101 begins rising to the left. When you reach a stop sign, turn right at Halleck Street, the run's four-mile mark. Continue west along the fence towards the Golden Gate Bridge.

This long, straight stretch, parallel to the Golden Gate Promenade, passes through Crissy Field, named for Major Dana Crissy, killed in the 1919 Transcontinental Air Race. These days it's seldom used as a landing strip. You'll next come to an impressive white building on the left, Stillwell Hall, housing Army Logistics Control. At the road's fenced end, go right onto Hamilton Street. This leads directly to the Fort Point Coast Guard Station. Turn left, then right around it and rejoin the Promenade. Here the surface changes to loose gravel and wind-blown sand for a short stretch before coming to the public fishing pier. Continue on the trail as it passes on wooden planks between two buildings. (On race day, out-bound runners are directed around this narrow path.)

It is now a clear run to Fort Point. You might get wet if you stay too close to the wall's edge because the breaking waves can be huge. Watch for surfers who sometimes gambol here. At the stone pillars marking the entrance to Fort Point, a path branches left, up to the Golden Gate Bridge. Continue through the parking lot and touch the brick wall of Fort Point, the turnaround. Fort Point was built on this northernmost promontory of the San Francisco peninsula between 1853 and 1861. It is the largest brick fortification ever built on the west coast, but it has never seen battle action. It served as a construction headquarters during the building of the Golden Gate Bridge and was also manned during World War II to watch for enemy submarines. In 1971, it became the first national park site in the Bay Area, and is now a museum.

On the run back, go past the Coast Guard station, without turning on Hamilton. You'll pass through a parking lot before spotting the clear Promenade trail. There are splendid views of ships on the bay, of the city's skyline, of Marin and the East Bay. The path is dirt until the asphalt resumes near the far end of the Parcourse. You'll reach the Water Quality Control Building, cross the parking lot in front of the St. Francis Yacht Club and run east toward the Marina Green. Open up your stride, if you'd like. The course ends at the flagpole midway along the south side of the Marina Green.

MARIN

Tennessee Valley

Distance: *3.45 miles*
Hills: *Gradual 190 feet climb*
Surface: *Mostly dirt, some asphalt*

Tennessee Valley, in just the few years it has been open to the public, has become a favorite among running courses in Marin County. It's easy to understand why. You run on a broad trail through verdant hills to the ocean in a sleepy, pastoral setting — one of the most pleasant trails in the Bay Area.

Follow Highway 101 north trom San Francisco four miles past the Golden Gate Bridge. Exit at the Mill Valley-Stinson Beach-Highway 1 turnoff. Turn left at the Tennessee Valley Road sign, which will appear soon; if you reach the traffic light at Almonte Blvd., you've missed your turn. (This spot is well served by Golden Gate Transit buses. Take any that pass Tam Valley Junction, such as routes 7 and 61 from the Sausalito ferry terminal.) Follow the paved road for a short while and you'll see the Golden Gate National Recreation Area sign for Tennessee Valley. You may want to park here if you're coming at a crowded time, or if you choose to add 1.3 miles to the run. Otherwise, continue on to the gate and park.

The run starts at the gate on the broad, paved Tennessee Valley Trail. While the whole trail drops some 200 feet to the ocean, this first part is the most noticeable downgrade. Use it to limber up both your body and mind. Thoughts of the city fade in this beautiful setting. In spring, the hills are ablaze with color, mostly from poppies and lupine.

After 1100 yards, the paved path gives way to dirt.

On the left is a private, working ranch. In another 350 yards, you'll come to a fork. One path is marked "Private Residence." Take it only if you're running soon after a rain, for the main trail can get quite muddy, even impassable. This route is a bit longer, and has an extra hill. Otherwise, go left along the fence, past the little wooden sign that marks the Tennessee Valley Trail.

You'll be following Tennessee Valley Creek. A few wooden planks cross it and 50 yards beyond is the run's one-mile point — easily recognized by the presence of a lone conifer surrounded by many willows. This is the potentially muddy stretch. You'll soon reach the intersection with the Pacific Coast Trail. Rodeo Beach and Muir Beach are equally 4.7 kilometers (2.9 miles) away, and both make fine, hilly runs. Press straight ahead. The higher trail rejoins yours from the right a quarter mile beyond. You may be dodging cows wandering on the

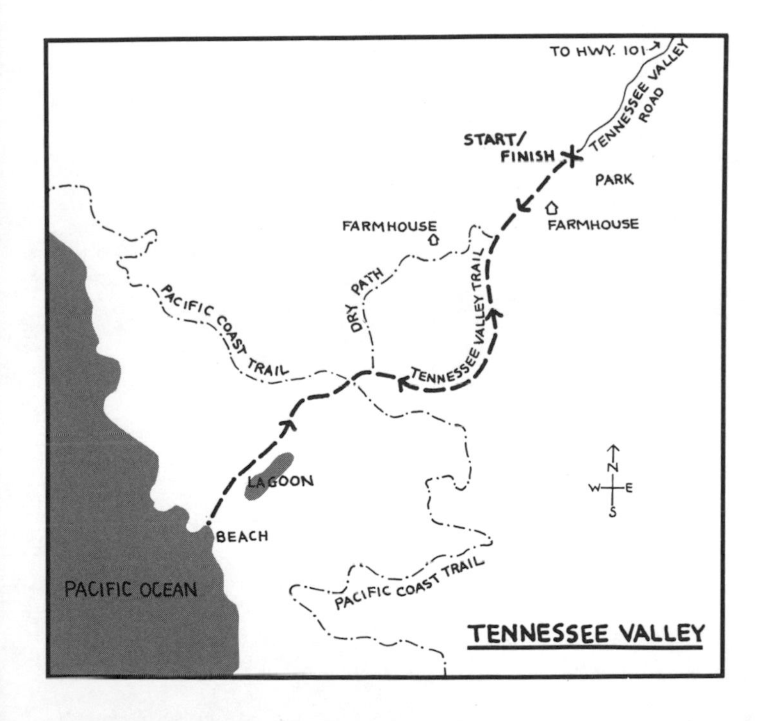

road here. And you'll be catching your first glimpses of the ocean.

Now you've come upon a lagoon, a favorite haunt of ducks in fall and winter. There are portable bathrooms nearby. Run to the lagoon's right, by a sign that warns of dangers ahead at high tide. Continue straight towards the ocean until the path gets sandy, then (surprise!) you're on the beach itself. It's a small cove but a striking one with rocky cliffs on both sides. The passenger ship "Tennessee" ran aground here in 1853. It'll almost surely be cool and windy. Roam at the ocean's edge if you like.

Return over the same path. If you found the trail too muddy, take the upper road. (Another alternative is the Wok-Mi Trail, which skirts the lagoon's southern edge before regaining the main path.) Join another runner to share the glorious scene. Just tackle that final hill to the finish.

Mt. Tamalpais

Distance: *3.7 miles*
Hills: *One of 300 feet, one of 250 feet*
Surface: *Dirt trails with gravel*

Standing 2571 feet at its highest point, Mt. Tamalpais dominates almost every vista in southern Marin. Its green, unspoiled slopes, laced with hundreds of trails, are a constant lure to runners. Tam offers enough variety, beauty and solitude to last a lifetime. This trail, on the northwest shoulder, offers an easy introduction to the mountain.

Take the Stinson Beach-Highway 1 exit from 101, just north of the Golden Gate Bridge. Follow Highway 1 (Shoreline Highway) for 3½ miles, then go right at the Muir Woods-Mt. Tamalpais turnoff. You're now on Panoramic Highway. Follow its ever-expanding vistas past the Muir Woods turnoff (1.3 miles), Mountain Home (3.0 miles), Bootjack Campground (5.5 miles), and the Pantoll Ranger Station (5.9 miles). At Pantoll, veer right, uphill. In 1.4 miles, you meet Ridgecrest Road. Cross it straight into the Rock Springs parking lot. This is the starting point. (Golden Gate Transit bus routes 62 and 63 stop at Pantoll.) From here, run the one-mile uphill on the Old Mine Trail to Rock Springs.

There are restrooms and drinking water inside the gate. Run uphill on Ridgecrest Road. Follow the paved road — which leads cars to the Tam summit — for 200 yards to the entrance of the Sidney B. Cushing Memorial Theatre, better known as the Mountain Theatre, used for plays in summer. Bear left to the amphitheatre. Run be-

On the slopes of Tamalpais

hind the top rows, as the views of Tiburon and beyond are splendid. Continue straight (there's no clear trail) and rejoin the highway directly in front of the well-marked Rock Springs-Lagunitas fire road. Join this broad path by scrambling over or veering around the highway bank. This is your farewell to cars, and on weekdays, probably to all people as well.

The first sign says that you're heading for Potrero Meadows. The Rock Springs-Lagunitas fire road is a rolling trail. It's mostly uphill and open to the course's crest of 2275 feet, reached .9 miles into the run. Then it's mostly a forested downhill. The loose rocks on the path can make it slippery, so be careful. Early on, to the left, you'll see a water tank with an outstretched pipe. Here, and from the many springs you'll pass on this run, the water — when it's flowing — is delicious.

A few hundred yards past the crest, you'll come to the first fork with a broad fire road. Veer left. Delightful

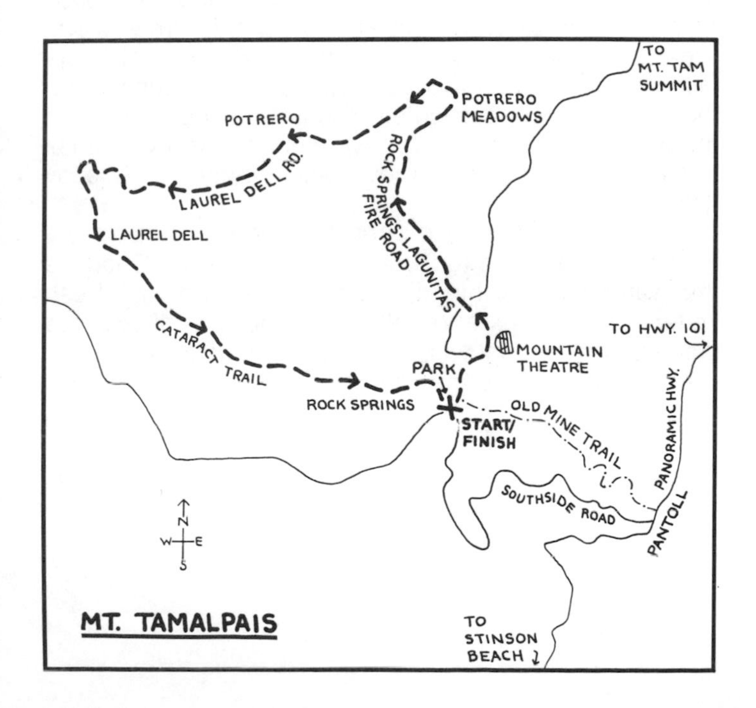

Potrero Meadows will be to your right and you'll see trail signs. You're heading towards Laurel Dell. Continue into the coolness of the forest. The trail is rolling, mostly downhill, with small streams at its margins. To the right is Potrero Camp, a favorite resting spot for horseback riders and hikers.

Suddenly, as you leave the forest, magnificent views unveil. On a clear day, you can see well beyond Bodega Head on the coast and beyond Mt. St. Helena inland. In winter, snowcapped peaks are visible 100 miles to the north. Below is Alpine Lake. Stretch your legs, for the trail is now almost entirely downhill, and soak in the glory of Tamalpais. You will return to the forest, meaning Laurel Dell is near.

A bathroom unceremoniously marks the dell amid a shaded picnic area. To the right are tables, a fountain, and the steep trail to Alpine Lake. You're 2.45 miles into the run. Continue straight and in 100 yards veer left off the fire trail. You'll cross a rivulet, entering the woods to the left of Cataract Creek. Follow this creek along Cataract Trail all the way back to Rock Springs. It's uphill, of course, a 300–foot gain in 1¼ miles of running. But the setting is cool and quiet. You'll run under, over, and through fallen trees, cross wooden planks over small streams, and encounter a few rocky patches — all easy to handle.

The first clearing means that you're nearing the finish. It's back then to Rock Springs Meadow. Opposite the water tank, within the cairn, is a pipe with fresh water. Take a drink and call it quits here. Or if you're a diehard, run the final yards back to the parking lot.

Welcome to the fraternity of Mt. Tamalpais runners!

Angel Island

Distance: *4.8 miles*
Hills: *Rolling*
Surface: *Mostly asphalt, some dirt*

A good argument could be made that the perimeter road around Angel Island is as ideal a running course as any in the Bay Area. It's a 4.8 mile loop around the island, with beautiful and ever-changing panoramas. You're always at the water's edge, so the air is temperate. The island itself is lovely, abundant in wildflowers and wildlife. The trail is broad, rolling, easy to follow and its surface is smooth. There are restrooms and fountains along the way. You'll encounter very few people and, perhaps best of all, there are no cars, except for a few official vehicles. You have to take a ferry, or private boat over, of course, but that's really an added bonus. So, let's run Angel Island.

There's weekend ferry service throughout the year from Tiburon and San Francisco, daily from June through Labor Day. The quicker and more frequent Tiburon ferry leaves from downtown Tiburon, off Main Street. Call (415) 435-2131 for more information. The San Francisco ferry leaves from Pier 43½ at the foot of Taylor Street. The number, also for details of the ferry from Berkeley, is (415) 546-2815. Or come in your own boat and dock in the cove. In any case, bring the family, a bathing suit, and a picnic lunch. And note the time when your last ferry leaves!

The ferries land on the island's northwest shore, at Ayala Cove, anchorage site of the first Europeans in San Francisco Bay under Juan Ayala in 1775. Follow the path past the bathrooms and snack bar. Stop at the park

View from Angel Island (Photo by Sandy Upson)

museum, so you can better understand what you're going to see on the island tour. Then walk up the path on the left, to the junction with the perimeter road. This is the start of the annual Angel Island Race, a charity run conducted by The Guardsmen. You'll follow the same course. It's AAU-certified at 4.8 miles, not the 5.0 miles (8.0 kilometers) that the park sign indicates. Still, these trail markers, found throughout the course, are helpful for keeping track of your progress.

Run to the left, clockwise around the island. The up–and–down pattern is quickly established; the entire course is rolling without any long uphill, downhill, or flat stretches. The first views are of the North Bay. The North Ridge Trail, extending to the 781–foot summit of Mt. Caroline Livermore, is on the right. Pass the island's northernmost spot, Point Campbell, and the views shift to the east. Below on the far left is Winslow Cove, one of several delightful, sheltered beaches ideal for a picnic after the run.

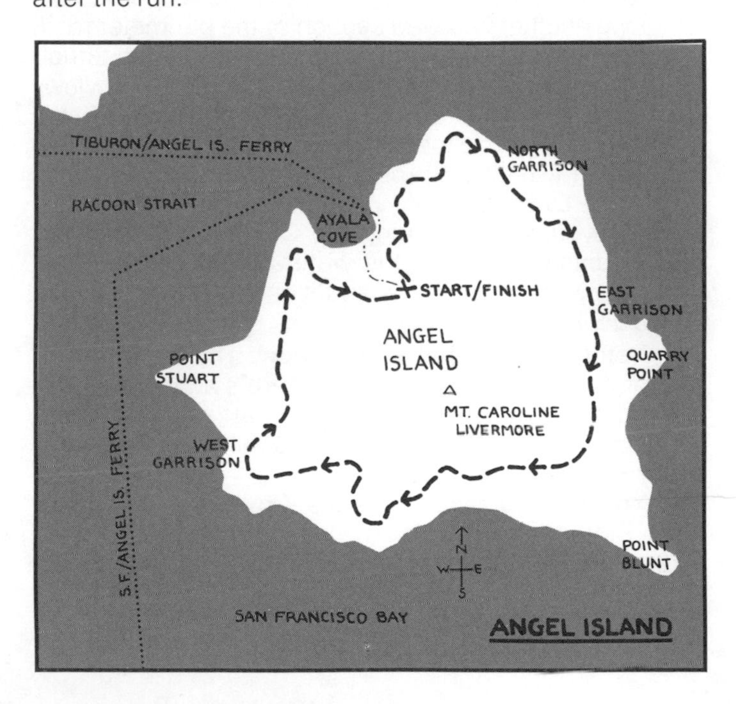

You then enter North Garrison, the western counterpart of New York's Ellis Island. Thousands of immigrants, mostly from Asia, entered the United States here. Then come good views of the Bay Bridge and Oakland. Next is downhill past the mostly abandoned buildings of East Garrison, or Fort McDowell. This was the chief U.S. military overseas processing station in the 1920s and 1930s, and housed prisoners of war during World War II. A path on the left leads to Quarry Beach, but stick to the perimeter road.

The road becomes dirt and gravel as you begin an uphill. From the summit is the first panorama of San Francisco. A path leads to the island's southeastern corner, Point Blunt, a Coast Guard station and the only part of the island not in the State Park. By the way, the tips of Point Blunt and Quarry Point are actually in the City and County of San Francisco. The next uphill reaches the course's summit of 290 feet. You'll feel the cooling breezes off the Golden Gate. At the three-way fork, veer left along another unpaved section of the perimeter road.

You'll pass a welcome water fountain by the turnoff for Battery Drew. Stay on the perimeter road. The views from the path are superb and there are seats at the cliff's edge if you want to pause. Next is an old quarry, so you're over two-thirds through. The paved road resumes at Battery Ledyard. Then you enter West Garrison, or Camp Reynolds, built during the Civil War. There's another fountain here, and the water-trough on the left is favored by some of the island's many (some say too many) deer.

You're on the final stretch now. The views are of Tiburon, across Racoon Strait. There's a last rise, then a wonderful downhill sprint to the start and finish line. The course record, incidentally, is 23 minutes, 7 seconds, set by Ron Wayne in 1976.

You can go back to Ayala Cove and the return ferry. Better yet, head back to your prearranged picnic spot where the cold drinks are waiting. Just don't forget that last ferry.

Marin Headlands

Distance: *4.9 miles*
Hills: *One of 830 feet over 2.1 miles*
Surface: *Half dirt trails, half asphalt*

This run is for real hill climbers, or for those who wish to become one. For your efforts, you'll get glorious views, a chance to run one of the best downhills in the Bay Area and a great workout. It will also introduce you to the Marin Headlands, the green hills just north of the Golden Gate.

From San Francisco, take the Alexander Avenue exit ¼ mile north of the Golden Gate Bridge. Following Alexander downhill about another ¼ mile, turn left on Bunker Road. This leads through a one-way tunnel — you wait until the traffic light is green before entering. Once through the tunnel, Bunker Road becomes the main artery along Rodeo Valley. Continue towards the ocean, noting your passage between Rodeo Lake and Rodeo Lagoon, where you'll be running soon. Just before the beach is the ranger station, where maps and information may be acquired. The main parking lot is just beyond; restrooms and water fountain are adjacent.

Although Muni provided buses out to Marin Headlands for a couple of summers, the service has been cancelled. GGNRA officials hope that public transit access to the Headlands will eventually be restored.

There may be crowds here on sunny and warm summer weekends. Don't worry. You'll soon be leaving most of the people behind. Pay a visit to the beach, if you like. You can comb the sand for jade and jasper fragments. And the surf is often spectacular.

Begin the run by following the road you just drove

in on. This is the only stretch with cars. Look for the abundant waterfowl, in fall and winter, on the lagoon. Indeed, this is one of the choicest birdwatching spots in the Bay Area. After .7 miles, the road reaches the bridge between the lake and the lagoon. Leave the road by staying to the left. You'll see a sign announcing the wildlife area, and another just beyond for the Miwok Trail.

Follow the dirt path. It might well be muddy here in winter. Bear with it, as the rest of the course will be much drier. You might see hang gliders, as this area is set aside for flying them. In .4 miles, you'll pass a trail leading back to the road. Shortly beyond is a real fork. Veer left, continuing on the marked Miwok Trail. And now comes the uphill, one of the toughest in this book.

It's an unbroken climb of 580 feet over this first 1.4 mile stretch. But the Miwok is a good trail to climb on — wide, peaceful, nicely graded, relatively smooth, and somewhat sheltered from the winds. In spring, the wildflowers are abundant here. You'll see fields of poppies, plus wild iris, lilies, and paintbrush.

After 1.4 miles, the trail passes next to a barbed wire fence. You'll see a white gate; it's unmistakable. Leave the Miwok Trail (which, by the way, continues to Muir Woods) by squeezing through the gate. You might be greeted by a cool gust of wind here. Take the Wolf

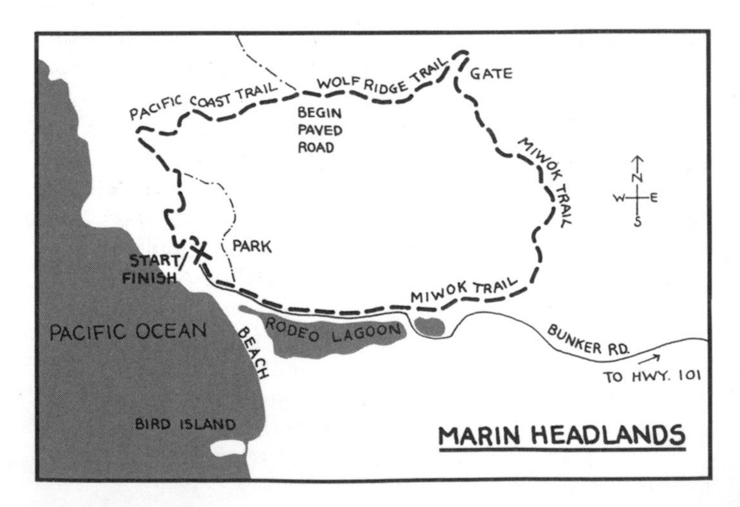

Ridge Trail to the left, along the fence. This is also your first, and all too brief, respite from the uphill.

This path, which you follow for .7 miles, is not quite as broad or as well graded as the Miwok, but it's still good running. There's an occasional downhill or level stretch, but you're mostly climbing for another 250 feet. The vistas are getting broader and you'll soon be quite alone here. There's a touch of poison oak around, so be cautious. If you hear some weird sounds, they're the much deflected moos from cows in Tennessee Valley below.

You might shudder a bit when you see the final push to the summit but press on. At the crest of 850 feet, the full panorama of San Francisco, Pacific Ocean, and Marin suddenly opens. You've made it! Cross to the paved road on your left. This is the Pacific Coast Trail, making a hairpin turn here. Uphill is the missile tracking site, closed to visitors. Take a deep breath (if you can!) and look at your watch (if you have one). Then blaze downhill.

It's 1.7 miles down, all paved and well graded, with cars forbidden. The panoramas are breathtaking, and they change around every turn. The ocean sparkles below. You and your legs will feel great. This is easily one of the best running stretches around. Fly! There's one intersection, two-thirds down, with another paved road. Veer right. Sooner than you've ever covered 1.7 miles, you're right back at the starting point.

Limantour Spit

Distance: *5.7 miles*
Hills: *None, flat*
Surface: *Sand*

Point Reyes National Seashore is among the grand treasures of northern California. It covers some 64,000 acres of a peninsula jutting into the Pacific, geologically separated from the Bay Area by the San Andreas Fault. The park includes over 50 miles of coastline, as well as mountain ridges, gently rolling hills, forests, lakes, bays, marshes and valleys. Much of the land is accessible only by trail. And all of the park, except for a few remaining private ranches, is free, and open to the public. Most loop run possibilities at Point Reyes are fairly arduous — long, and with major hill work. So as an introduction, you'll run a flat up-and-back course along Limantour Spit, with a dramatic turn-around point.

From San Francisco, follow Highway 101 for nine miles north of the Golden Gate Bridge to the Sir Francis Drake Boulevard exit. Follow Sir Francis Drake some 25 miles through the towns of central Marin, into the pastoral area beyond Fairfax, through Samuel Taylor State Park, and finally, to the intersection with Highway 1 at Olema. Go right and, in less than ¼ mile, take a left at the large Point Reyes National Seashore sign. You'll pass the park's headquarters at Bear Valley, the focal point of many trails. About a mile farther is the left turn onto Limantour Road — eight lovely miles to the ocean. Park in the lot at the road's end. (Golden Gate Transit bus #64 from San Francisco stops at the Bear Valley

Headquarters. Then hop the free Park Service shuttle bus that leaves Bear Valley for Limantour Beach every half hour from 10 a.m. to 5 p.m. on summer weekends.)

There are bathrooms and a fountain below the parking lot towards the beach. Your starting point is the dirt trail that branches to the right just past the lagoons. This trail makes for easier running than beginning directly on the sand. Follow this straight path west. To the right is Estero de Limantour, alive with waterfowl in the winter. Peregrine falcons, rare anywhere in the world, have even been sighted here in their 180 mph dive for shorebirds. Incredibly, a residential development was once begun here. You can still see traces of the building sites among the dunes. A few lonely trees dot the road. When the path ends, veer left towards the beach and continue running west.

You're actually on Drake's Bay. Many maintain that Sir Francis Drake first sighted it in 1579, although his exact landing site remains the greatest puzzle in California history. More certain is Sebastian Cermeno's visit to this beach in 1595. This is a wild and magnificent stretch. The sand is clean and untouched. The chances of meeting anyone out here are unlikely, and they become less with every stride. Look for seals, dolphins, and scoters offshore, as well as migrating gray whales. The area is known also as a breeding ground for sharks. Ahead, in the distance, looms Point Reyes itself.

Run where it's easiest, near the water's edge, to the end of the Spit. This is a very special place, with water on three sides and the long, lonely beach behind. White pelicans are often visible across the channel leading to Drake's Estero. Drake's Beach is off to the left. Linger here, even if you usually don't stop when running. This is a spot to be cherished.

Begin the long run back along the beach. Though running on sand is tiring, you'll probably want to continue on the beach all the way. The only tricky part is spotting where the road to the parking lot is. Look for a break in the dunes about .4 mile past the first cluster of refuse cans. If you run slightly past or short, just scramble over the dunes and you'll spot the parking area.

Marin Lakes

Distance: *7.2 miles*
Hills: *One of 100 feet, another of 575 feet*
Surface: *Dirt trails*

There are five major lakes — Alpine, Bon Tempe, Kent, Lagunitas, and Phoenix — nestled in the ridges north and west of Mt. Tamalpais. The lakes serve as reservoirs for Marin County, and this entire area of almost unspoiled wilderness is open to the public. But access by car is very limited. Thankfully, the many trails are for hikers and runners only.

You can run from one lake to the next, around the lakes, south to the Mt. Tamalpais trails, or west towards the ocean. In short, the area is a runner's paradise. This trail is easily accessible at its start, passes three of the lakes and close to a fourth, has a gradual, beginning uphill, and is shaded by trees over 90 percent of the way. Sound good? Give it a try.

Take the San Anselmo–Sir Francis Drake exit off Highway 101 about nine miles north of the Golden Gate. Follow Sir Francis Drake Boulevard west for five miles to the first traffic light in the town of Ross. Go left up Lagunitas Road. It leads, in ¾ mile, to Natalie Coffin Greene Park. It's another ⅓ mile to the parking area. If the lot is filled, park along Lagunitas and enjoy the added run. Several Golden Gate Transit buses pass the Sir Francis Drake-Lagunitas Road intersection, such as the #20 from San Francisco and the free feeder bus from the Larkspur ferry terminal. There are bathrooms and a fountain at the start.

Start running uphill past the gate marked "Protection

Road." You'll reach the Phoenix Lake spillway — hopefully, overflowing in the spring — after gaining 100 feet in elevation. At the crest is the lake itself. Pass the park residence and circle the lake counterclockwise on a level trail. Phoenix is the most visited of the lakes, popular with fishermen and hikers.

Past a second park residence, the trail goes due west to Phoenix Junction, the one–mile mark. You face a choice of three trails. To the left is the most direct way to Mt. Tamalpais' summit. Straight ahead is the return trail on this loop. For now, go right on the Shaver Grade fire road.

This is a well–graded path along tree-lined Phoenix Creek that ascends 575 feet in 1.9 miles. You'll probably have the trail all to yourself. A small trail goes to the right, and a larger one is on the left. Soon you'll reach the major trail intersection of Five Corners. Continue on Shaver Grade by taking the extreme left-hand road.

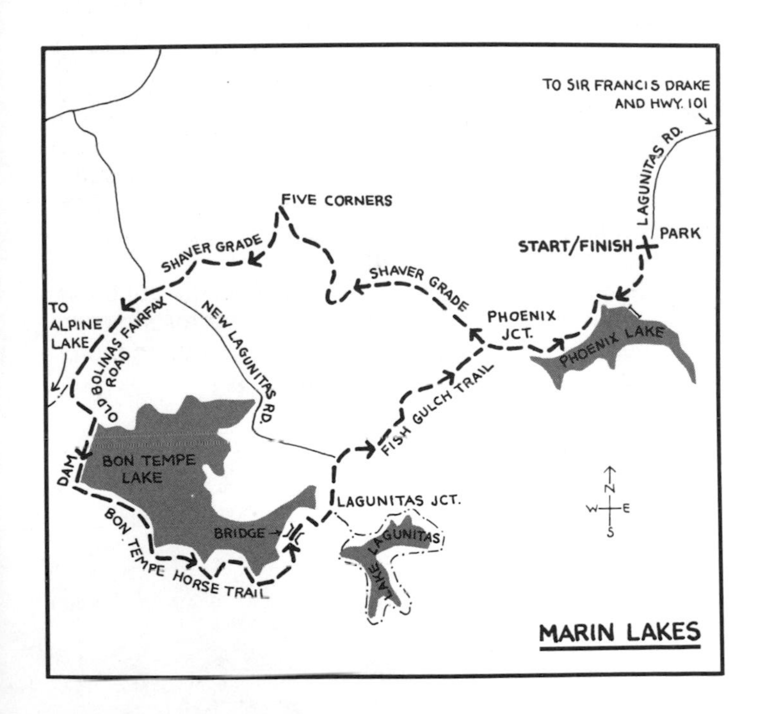

At last, at the paved road, you reach the run's highest point of 775 feet. Cars aren't allowed to enter on Tuesdays, making it the quietest day for a run. Cross the road straight onto a small dirt horse trail. It leads quickly to a dirt and gravel downhill road. Follow it, then go left at the Bon Tempe sign. Alpine Lake is visible straight ahead. Pass the parking area, the bathrooms, and the lake's spillway. You'll now cross the dam, with Bon Tempe Lake shimmering to the left. Beyond the dam — skirting another bathroom — go left onto the trail that circles Bon Tempe.

This is an excellent running path — soft, peaceful and shaded. Follow it counterclockwise along the lake for 1½ miles, across three wooden bridges, over some easy rolling terrain, and past many channelled rivulets. You round the lake's treeless southwest corner, then you soon reach Lagunitas Junction. Cross the bridge and go right. Straight ahead and uphill is Lagunitas Lake, which can be circled for two extra miles of running. Proceed left on the dirt road leading away from the parking lot.

You'll meet the paved road again. Veer right. It's all downhill now, and free from cars. Run left at the fork towards Phoenix Lake, not the filter plant. This is Fish Gulch Road, somewhat steeper than the path you came up on but every bit as tranquil. You can really get in some fast downhill cross-country running here. Just be wary of the steep creek bank to the left.

In a few minutes, you're back at Phoenix Junction. Continue straight on the same path you've already run, retracing your steps around the lake. You'll descend on the same road back to the parking lot.

Tiburon Loop

Distance: *8.6 miles*
Hills: *One of 110 feet, otherwise gently rolling*
Surface: *Asphalt*

The annual race around Tiburon, revived in 1978, has always been among the loveliest on the running circuit. This run makes a complete loop around the Tiburon Peninsula — first on its rolling, isolated northeast shore, then through Tiburon itself, and finally back on an excellent running trail at water's edge.

Take the Tiburon exit off 101, six miles north of the Golden Gate. Follow Tiburon Boulevard east for 1.6 miles, until it narrows to two lanes. Then turn right at Greenwood Beach Road and park in the dirt lot known as Blackie's Pasture — named after the horse that once grazed there. (He's buried in the white-fenced plot.) There's Golden Gate Transit bus service from the Tiburon ferry terminal via Route #9, or directly from San Francisco and Sausalito weekdays on Route #10.

Walk back to Tiburon Boulevard and carefully cross it. Take the footpath towards Tiburon. After 150 yards, run left onto Trestle Glen Boulevard. Here the hill begins almost immediately. It's ½ mile long and 110 feet up. Run easily; you want to still be fresh at the top. At the hill's crest is the intersection with Paradise Drive. A left turn leads to Corte Madera. You veer right. That's the last turn for nearly eight miles.

Paradise Drive is gently rolling throughout its length. About the biggest commotion you'll hear is made by the Larkspur Ferry as it plies San Francisco Bay. There'll be very few cars on the road, but still be cautious, particularly around curves. The run's one-mile mark is at the

4.55 mile highway road sign, the two–mile mark is at 5.55 miles, and so on.

You'll soon pass Paradise Beach County Park on the left, an ideal spot for swimming and picnicking. The views are getting broader, a full panorama of the north of San Francisco Bay. The next landmark is the Tiburon Center for Environmental Studies, administered by San Francisco State University. Across from it is Tiburon Uplands County Park. Leave the water's edge for awhile and return by Kiel Cove.

The last highway marker reads 8.63 miles, so you've run 5.1 miles. There is then a short rise to reach the Tiburon line. The houses are more compact, but the view doesn't suffer. Angel Island beckons just across Racoon Strait, and now comes a glorious, refreshing downhill. Stretch your legs out. It will feel good and help you over the remaining miles. The bottom of the hill is alongside the water.

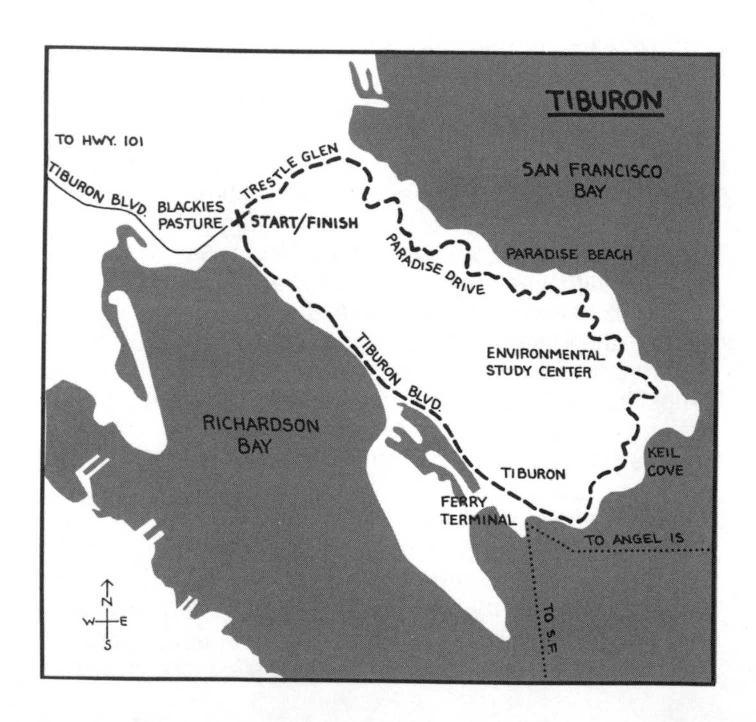

Cross Tiburon's colorful Main Street. Paradise Drive is now called Tiburon Boulevard. This is the only crowded section of the run. Watch for cars going in and out of the parking areas. Join the bicycle path on the left. The first mileage marker on it is 2.250, painted in white on both sides of the path, just past Beach Road. So there's 2¼ miles to go, all level.

Soon your path veers left, away from Tiburon Boulevard, and the running is ideal. Run on either the asphalt or the dirt. You'll see other runners, bicyclists, and strollers on the trail. They add to the pleasant atmosphere. Beyond Belvedere, the path is again right by Richardson Bay. This is a wildlife sanctuary and the ducks know it. You enter Richardson Bay Park, but you won't notice any difference.

You decide when you feel comfortable enough to begin picking up the pace. With 300 yards to go, the path forks. Go downhill, towards the water. At last, the final sprint is here — past the sewage treatment plant, then over the bridge and back to the parking lot.

You've earned a rest. Afterwards, try Paradise Beach for a swim or downtown Tiburon for shopping, or the Audubon Center just up Greenwood Beach Road for some birdwatching.

EAST BAY

Lafayette Reservoir

Distance: *2.78 miles*
Hills: *Gently rolling*
Surface: *Asphalt*

The East Bay Municipal Utility District (EBMUD) administers some 27,000 acres in the East Bay hills, concentrated around five reservoirs — Briones, Chabot, Lafayette, San Pablo, and Upper San Leandro. Most of this relatively unspoiled land, which allegedly still contains mountain lions, was closed to the public until 1973. Now the runner has access to many miles of trails.

You'll take the loop trail around Lafayette Reservoir as an introduction to EBMUD lands. It offers several advantages. For one, it is the easiest circuit of any of the reservoirs. Indeed, Briones is the only other lake that can be looped on regular trails — and that course is 14 miles long. Also, no trail permit is required at Lafayette. (These permits, available at any EBMUD office, should be carried when taking other district trails.) Finally, the Lafayette course is paved, making it ideal for running in the rainy season.

Take Highway 24 east through the Caldecott Tunnel to the first Lafayette exit, Mount Diablo Boulevard. Continue east one mile to the reservoir entrance on the right. A BART station is to the east in downtown Lafayette. To save the $1 auto fee, park on the road shoulder across the street. It's a ¼ mile uphill run to the loop trail. Otherwise, drive up and park in the huge lot to the left. There are bathrooms and fountains throughout the course.

You'll start where the popular 10 kilometer race begins — up the small left-hand rise by the entrance to the Rim Trail. There's a lovely meadow here for stretching

A sunny day at Lafayette Reservoir

before or after the run. (A few words first about the Rim Trail, which offers a much tougher alternative course. It's quite hilly and you may soon be on all fours scrambling up one of its most notorious hills, nicknamed Mt. Everest. The distance for the almost-complete circle of the reservoir is listed at 4.7 miles, but it's actually a little longer. Try the Rim Trail, also the site of an annual race, when you're in the mood for rugged cross-country running.)

Start in a counterclockwise direction around the reservoir, retracing your steps down the incline and over the dam in front of the parking lot. The tower looms out of the only part of the lake closed to boaters. You pass the fish-cleaning area, an elevated picnic site, and the exit from the loop around the Rim Trail. Next is a descent into the park's busiest area. There may be youngsters lining the banks here, either fishing or feeding the waterfowl.

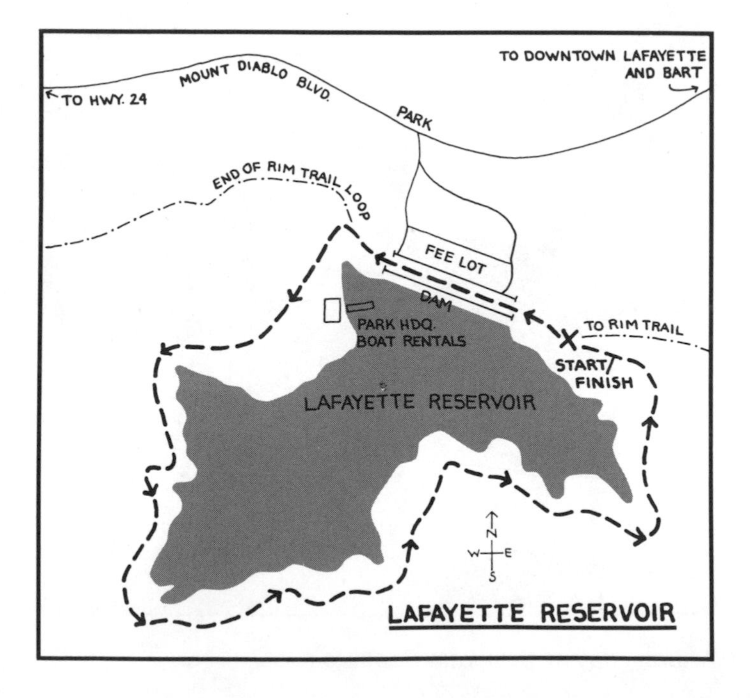

Keep straight, passing the boat rental building. This short uphill shouldn't bother you now but you'll sure notice it if you race here. The 10 kilometer finish line (after two laps, plus the distance from your starting point) is cruelly placed at the crest. You'll pass a meadow, and leave all cars behind. The blacktop path is gently rolling all the way around the reservoir. Though there's occasional shade from the oak trees, the path is mostly through open chaparral. Even with the gentle breeze off the water, it's usually hot here on summer days.

You'll pass several more access paths to the Rim Trail and run by numerous shaded picnic areas. There are changing views of the reservoir and in the distance, glimpses of Mt. Diablo. Relax, say hello to the other runners and enjoy the scenery. You'll spot the starting area, but it's not as close as you think because the path must first loop around the long southeastern arm of the reservoir.

You've run 2.78 miles, not the 2.7 miles listed in the park brochure. You can run another loop, or head up to the Rim Trail, or rent a rowboat, or try some fishing, or picnic on the grass or tables. Express yourself. There's even a large cooking spit, good for a luau, to the left of the meadow.

Lake Merritt

Distance: *3.05 miles*
Hills: *None, flat*
Surface: *Asphalt, hardened dirt*

Perhaps the single most popular running course in the Bay Area is Lake Merritt, in the heart of Oakland. You can go almost anytime and be cheered as the steady stream of runners, from plodders to champions, passes by. The course's popularity is understandable. It's easily accessible, flat, attractive, and there's so much else to do nearby for you and the family.

You can start anywhere, of course. But since Lake Merritt is the oldest waterfowl refuge in the United States, the best place to start is where most of the birds roost. That spot is the Rotary Natural Science Center, on Merritt's northeast shore. There are bathrooms and fountains available.

By car, take the Grand Avenue exit west from Highway 580 about ½ mile, then turn left on Perkins and park by the lake. AC Transit bus Route B — to and from San Francisco — stops at Perkins and Grand. BART has two stations within a few blocks of the lake — the 19th Street stop to the west and the Lake Merritt stop to the south.

This course is measured from the golden eagle cage by the main entrance to the Science Center. Since there's talk of removing these cages, look for the big aviary, the first geodesic dome built in America. Run clockwise, always sticking to the lake's edge. As you'll notice, there's much bird activity around. The Canada geese, snowy and great egrets, and black crowned night herons are among the more exotic species that nest here. Some of Oakland's finest buildings also ring the

Oakland's skyline across Lake Merritt

lake — like the Women's Athletic Club just past the children's playground. Soon you'll reach the ivy-covered pagoda called El Embarcadero, an old-time boat dock. The one-mile mark is at the sign for East 18th Street, across from 1830 Lakeshore.

Next you'll cross the 12th Street Dam, which connects the lake to the Oakland Estuary. It's a popular spot with fishermen. Most runners stick to the shoreline by taking the path down across from the Oakland Auditorium, so you'll do the same. The Alameda County Court House and the main Oakland public library are two other civic buildings here. Nearer the lake is the old Camron-Stanford House, once home of the Oakland Museum.

Next, on the right, is the old boathouse. Most races around the lake begin here. It's also the focal point for the championship crew races held on Lake Merritt. On the left is the Scottish Rite Temple. The run's two-mile point is at the foot of Jackson Street, and there's a

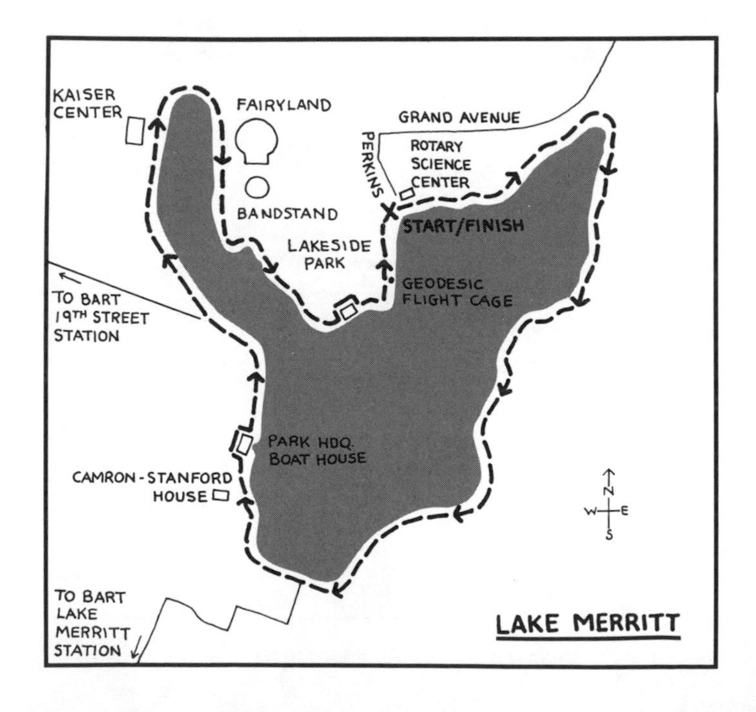

marker painted on the path a few feet beyond.

To the left soars the gently curved Kaiser Center. Loop back south again and just uphill is Fairyland, where adults are admitted only if accompanied by a child. Very civilized! Again take the shortest route, over a short stretch of sand, and pass the colonnaded bandstand, the scene of many Sunday afternoon concerts. There's a tiny hill and the Lakeside Horticultural Center, famous particularly for the chrysanthemum displays.

You're in Lakeside Park now. Follow another shortcut and, to the right, is the blue Sailboat House. Once past the food stand, you're on the home stretch. If it isn't too crowded, race beyond the three-mile mark and back to the starting point.

Now you've plenty of amusements to choose from. You could rent a sailboat or rowboat, visit the Science Center, take the kids to Fairyland, have a picnic, view the gardens, or (alas!) take another loop.

Redwood Regional Park

Distance: *4.2 miles*
Hills: *One of 565 feet*
Surface: *Dirt*

Redwood Regional Park's 2,229 acres offer a rich variety of running trails. Indeed, along with adjacent Anthony Chabot Regional Park and Oakland's Joaquin Miller Park, this area is rivalled in the Bay Area only by Mt. Tamalpais for running possibilities. Your loop course will include some wonderful views and a long stretch through the redwoods.

From the Bay Bridge, follow Highway 580 south four miles to the Fruitvale Avenue exit. Pass Fruitvale and turn left on Lincoln Avenue. Follow it uphill to Highway 13, where Lincoln becomes Joaquin Miller Road. In another mile, past Joaquin Miller Park, go left on Skyline Boulevard. After 1¼ miles, take a right into the park (10900 Skyline) at the sign for the Redwood Bowl and Archery Range. Park in the free, large lot in front of the Redwood Bowmen Archery Range. This is the park's Sequoia Gate. The main entrance, the Redwood Gate, is several miles to the southeast off Redwood Road. A parking fee is charged there. AC Transit bus 15A stops nearby at the Roberts Recreation Area.

Start your run on the West Ridge Trail, marked in yellow on a concrete barrel to the right of the lot. You immediately pass a residence and a water fountain to the left. Just beyond, again to the left, are the archery range and bathrooms. The trail continues along the floor of the Redwood Bowl, a popular spot for picnicking and frisbee tossing. Pass the gate and you'll be at a trail junction. Next veer left on the Ridge Trail. (After the run, though, you may want to head towards the heated public swimming pool in the Thomas J. Roberts area on your right.) You begin to get a taste of the vistas ahead. Quickly, the Madrone Trail comes in from the left. Later, you will complete your loop on it. For now, continue on the Ridge Trail. If you're running late in the afternoon, you might want to reverse the direction of the loop — getting more light while in the forest and then watching the sunset from the ridge.

The eucalyptuses give way to chaparral and splendid views of the Bay. The broad trail—which can be dusty in late summer and muddy in early spring—is rolling but generally downhill. The unmarked Baccharis Trail enters on your right. Then the narrow Fern Trail emerges from the left. After 1¼ miles, go left on the well-marked Sidney Chown Trail. Those who want a longer run of 5¼ miles, continue to the next downhill trail, the Orchard Trail.

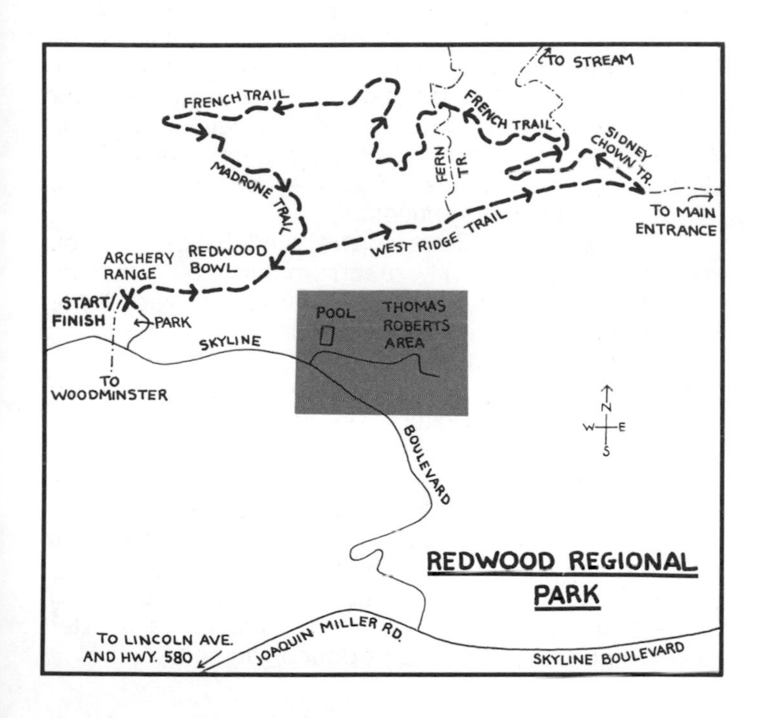

The Chown Trail quickly enters rich foliage and its descent, a total of 215 feet, becomes more gradual. The path is narrow — single file only — as you enter the redwood forest. Soon comes a trail junction and a wooden post marking the East Bay Skyline National Recreation Trail. Eventually this trail will extend some 30 miles from Alvarado Park in Richmond to Castro Valley's Don Castro Park. The trail has two branches in Redwood Park — the West Ridge which you just covered and the French Trail which you now take left.

A lovely trail, you run on a soft path amidst the cool and quiet redwoods. These are second-growth trees. The original giants — one was documented at 31½ feet in diameter — were extensively cut in the 1840s and 1850s, when the area was a major logging center. In fact, there were four sawmills, complete with loggers' towns, within the present park boundaries.

This solitary trail starts out mostly level. You'll see another Skyline Trail sign, where the Fern Trail crosses your path. Hop over an occasional log and enjoy! The French Trail becomes uphill. You'll cross the Mill Trail and hit a steep 100-yard section, followed by another 50-yard hill. At the next intersection, veer left, uphill. You begin a long, steady climb back to the West Ridge. Just take it nice and easy. Pass the Peak Trail junction on your right and keep chugging.

Finally, the uphill eases at a windy ridge, and you veer right. You'll quickly reach another trail junction. It's just a few yards to the left back to the West Ridge Trail. Retrace your steps to the start.

One last note. A special event occurs every Tuesday evening during summer in nearby Joaquin Miller Park. A group of runners — including many well-known personalities — gathers in the meadow below the Woodminster Theater to run the route of the annual Woodminster Race. It is 9¼ miles, passes this run's starting point, and includes one of the toughest hills found on any Bay Area race course. Afterwards, everyone shares in a splendid barbecue and picnic. All runners are welcome, even if you just run a shorter route. Bring some food and introduce yourself.

Point Pinole

Distance: *4.6 miles*
Hills: *Slight grades*
Surface: *Dirt and gravel trails, asphalt*

Point Pinole Regional Park occupies 2,147 acres of a peninsula jutting into San Pablo Bay from the northwest tip of Contra Costa County. It has gentle hills, tall eucalyptus groves, over four miles of shoreline, no cars (at all!), and sweeping vistas of Marin County and the North Bay. It also has several trails ideal for running and you'll encounter very few people on them since the park is still rather unknown. Point Pinole makes particularly good running on hot days because you can almost surely count on cool bay breezes.

In Richmond, take the Hilltop Drive exit west from Highway 80. Past the shopping center, take a right (north) onto San Pablo Avenue. Quickly look left for Atlas Road. Continue to Giant Road, where a left turn leads you directly to the park entrance. There's limited free parking on the roadside. AC Transit bus #78 serves the park from the Richmond BART station. Pick up a trail map at the ranger booth. There are bathrooms, but no fountains at the start (there is water, though, at the run's halfway mark). A shuttle service (50¢ fee) to the fishing pier at the park's other end begins here.

Begin running on the paved main trail, gently uphill. Cross the new bridge over the active Southern Pacific Railroad tracks and go left until you reach a fence. Then follow the dirt path to the right on the bluff above the beach. This is a good running trail; softened by grass and eucalyptus leaves, and passing over the remnants of an old narrow gauge railway. But run along the beach, if you prefer, though it's rocky. The beach path and yours meet just before the pier.

Stay on the cliff's edge trail at each intersection and you can't get lost. The views to the left across San Pablo Bay are splendid — the mountainous backbone of Marin, topped by Mt. Tamalpais, is clearly visible. To the right, up the grassy slopes, are the park's highest points. The one–mile mark is at the very first eucalyptus on the left. Those mysterious-looking wooden structures and concrete bunkers that you see are remnants of the Atlas Powder Works, which produced explosives on this site from 1880 to 1960. The loud bangs you hear are not, however, leftovers from the plant. They're from the skeet shooters at the nearby Richmond Rod and Gun Club.

The path emerges from the trees along the point's northern edge. Heed the many cliff markers and work your way gently down to sea level by the modern fishing

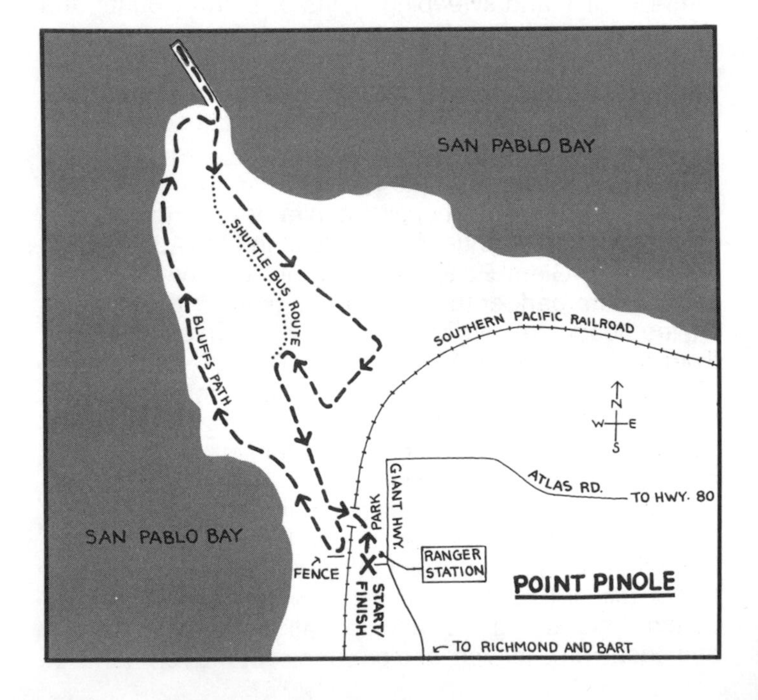

pier. This is the run's two–mile mark. Take a jaunt to the pier's end, a little over 400 yards each way. There are fountains on the pier, and lots of fishermen.

Back from your trip over the water, you'll see where the shuttle ends its circuit. There are fountains, bathrooms, and a picnic area. Look for the gravel path that takes off to the left. This will be your return route. It's level running on this little-used trail, much of it shaded by eucalyptus. There is a four-way intersection in just over a mile. Continue straight on the asphalt path, which doubles back to rejoin the main shuttle route. Veer left and you'll soon spot the bridge. Cross it and sprint the final downhill back to the parking lot.

Got your fishing pole? Then hop the shuttle back to the pier and catch tonight's dinner.

Alameda Creek — Coyote Hills

Distance: *5.9 miles*
Hills: *Half-rolling, half-flat*
Surface: *Asphalt*

The southern shoreline of the East Bay, long used primarily for the production of salt, has seen little residential development. The protection continues to this day, as much of the area has become part of a National Wildlife Refuge. Thus, a trail network through large open areas of Bay land is opening to the runner. One section already part of the East Bay Regional Park District is Coyote Hills Regional Park and the nearby Alameda Creek Trail. There's good running here all year — paved for the rainy season, cooled by breezes in the warm months.

Follow Highway 17 south to the Jarvis Avenue exit in Newark. In 1.2 miles, go right on Newark Boulevard. You'll pass the Coyote Hills Regional Park turnoff in a mile, but continue straight another .6 miles to a bridge, and the Alameda Creek Trail, at Lowry Road. There's a free parking lot just over the bridge to the left. Walk back over the bridge and down to the trail, your starting point. Unfortunately, there is no close public transportation. The Union City BART station is about a mile north of the Alameda Creek Trail on Decoto Road, three miles upstream from here.

The Alameda Creek Regional Trail currently stretches some 11 flat miles from the Bay to the mouth of Niles Canyon, and there are plans to extend it all the way to Sunol Regional Park. There are actually two parallel trails — the dirt and gravel one on the north side intended for horses, and the paved southern one for bicyclists. Runners and hikers may use either, but since the Newark Boulevard bridge is the last one before the Bay, you'll not be able to enter Coyote Hills unless you run on the bike path.

Begin running towards the Bay, southwest, on the asphalt trail. As the sign says, you are 1.6 miles from Coyote Hills Regional Park — the headquarters, not the park boundary. The water on your right is not Alameda Creek but a flood control channel leading to the Bay. The trail does join Alameda Creek, though, 1½ miles in the other direction. The channel is tidal, richest with birdlife when the water's low. There are presently no mileage indicators on this section — though it's expected that the quarter-mile posts found upstream on the trail will be added here as well.

After 1.2 miles, veer left at the Coyote Hills Regional

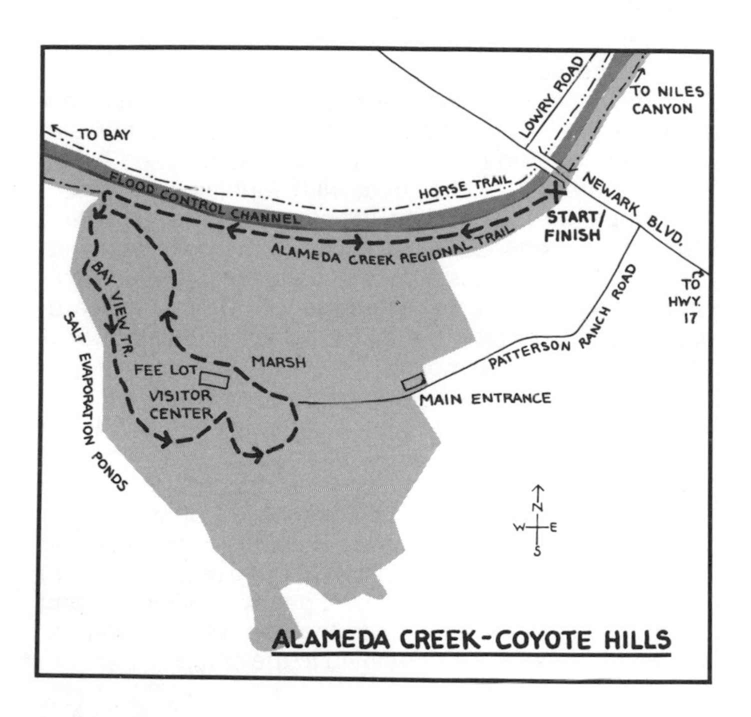

Park sign. You'll quickly meet a broad bike path with a white line down the middle. This is the Bay View Trail, and you'll follow it to the right, counterclockwise around the Park. The terrain is gently rolling, without any real hills. You'll see yellow mileage markers each quarter-mile on the pavement. They're not for your course nor were they painted for the Park, but they're still helpful for noting your progress.

The path veers south along the water. This section contains one of the largest concentrations of shorebirds and waterfowl in the Bay Area. It's really a fantastic sight in winter, and heartwarming to know that so much wildlife still remains here. Two of the most striking birds are slender waders — the Avocet with its upturned bill and buff-colored head, and the red-legged raucous Black Necked Stilt. You'll see the salt evaporation ponds of the Leslie Salt Company. The reddish tinge, so noticeable to plane travellers, is due to the algae, which nourishes huge quantities of brine shrimp. Intrepid runners can venture out onto these long levees that extend towards the water.

The path loops inland — you can't lose it if you follow the white line — and climbs a bit. You'll notice a mistake in the yellow markers — 3¼ miles is succeeded by 4½ miles. There's a picnic area, with fountains and bathrooms, below to the right. Continue past a gate and through a parking lot. You'll come to the main road into the park. Just across is a parallel path along the Alameda Creek Ponding Area. Take it to the left. There are boardwalks leading towards the marsh, which contains a 2500-year-old Indian shell mound.

You'll next pass the Park Headquarters area, with delightful shaded picnic spots (as you've noticed, there are no trees along the route), bathrooms, fountains and trail maps. (One reason it's best not to start here is the parking fee, which is $2 on weekends, $1 on weekdays. But if you run often in East Bay Regional Parklands, you might consider buying an annual parking permit for $25.) Rejoin the bike path and follow it gently uphill to the end of the park loop. Head back to the start by rejoining the Alameda Creek Trail and running to the bridge.

You'll probably want to return and further explore the Alameda Creek Trail. Pick up a map, decide what distance you want to run, park along the route, and run the trail to your heart's content.

Strawberry Canyon

Distance: *7.5 miles*
Hills: *685 foot gain from start to turnaround*
Surface: *Dirt*

There is a splendid running trail that winds through pristine Strawberry Canyon, on University of California land, in the forested hills east of the main campus. The course has become so popular among runners that the blackberries and other shrubs at the trail's edge have a noticeable coat of dust in summer. In the run's upper half, there are magnificent views. And the climate is right — the ridge above shields the canyon from winds and the summer heat.

To reach the trailhead, take the University Avenue exit east off Highway 80 in Berkeley. Follow University to its end on Oxford Street at the campus gate. Go left two blocks, then right on Hearst Avenue. In ¾ miles, go right on Gayley Road. Then take the first left onto Rimway, passing above Memorial Stadium. Finally, go left onto Centennial Drive. You'll pass athletic fields, tennis courts (last chance for water) and swimming pools (for the university community only). Then enter the first parking lot on your right. The free Humphrey Go-Bart shuttle bus from the downtown Berkeley BART station passes here.

If a 7.5 mile round trip run with a 685 foot elevation gain sounds like too much, you can run half the distance, all downhill, by pooling cars. Leave a car at the parking lot, then drive up Centennial to Grizzly Peak Boulevard. The trail emerges and you'll begin running to the right, at the fire trail gate beyond the Space Sciences Laboratory. There's some parking on the road shoulder but most runners use, in evenings and on weekends, the lab parking lot.

Ready to run? A small path leads, right of the stone wall, into the Ecological Study Area and the start of your broad, dirt running trail. Enter the moist, inviting forest. You'll quickly cross branches of Strawberry Creek which, fed by underground streams, runs all year. To your left is the fence that keeps the deer out of the renowned University Botanical Garden, with its huge collections of rhododendrons, roses, cacti and other plants. You're gaining elevation gradually. There are lots of runners here. You get the feeling a Nobel Prize laureate has just whizzed by downhill, and you might be right!

After about a mile, and a 200-foot rise, the path emerges at a quiet residential street, Panoramic Way, overlooking the campus. This is the end of the lower fire trail. You can take either of the two steep paths that continue upward to the left. They meet in a couple of hundred

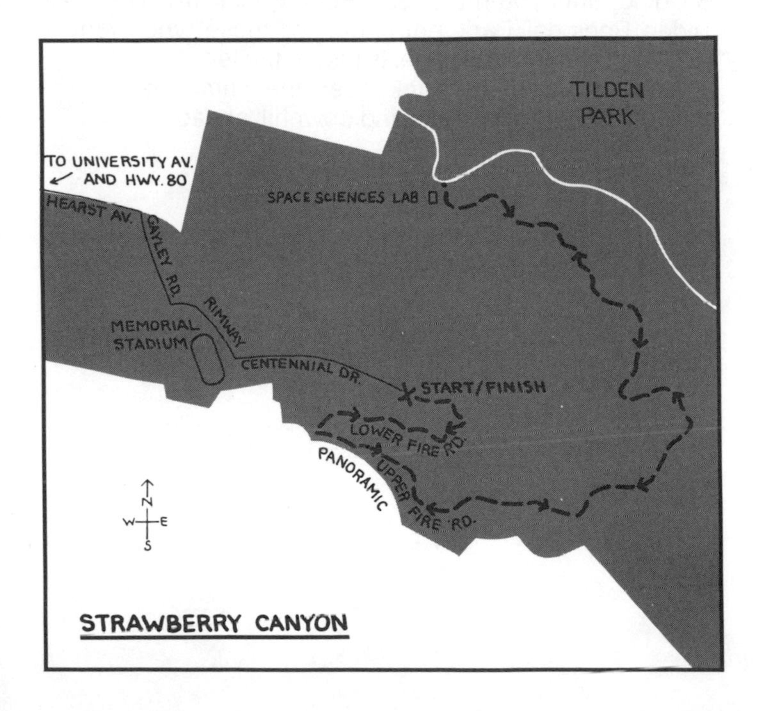

yards at the end of this stiffest uphill of the route. You're again by the edge of a street and the start of the upper fire trail. By the way, you're in Oakland now.

The path winds gently uphill, then levels off. To the left, between clearings in the eucalyptus, you can see the buildings nestled in the canyon below. They're mostly part of Berkeley's atomic energy complex, such as the domed cyclotron. But the old buildings beside the switchback road are certainly different — they housed experimentally-bred, prize chickens until a Berkeleyite's escaped pet ocelot, a gift from the Shah of Iran no less, wiped out the collection one night! As the road turns, you get tremendous vistas stretching from the San Mateo Bridge to San Francisco and the Golden Gate, and to Mt. Tamalpais and beyond. Or you might see the fog rolling in, or nothing but the fog.

Savor this long, lovely stretch. Finally you'll notice another uphill. Keep climbing past the Space Sciences Building, until you hit Grizzly Peak Boulevard. The main Tilden Regional Park entrance, for those who want to really get in some mileage, is just to the left.

For now, head back over the same route. The trail, of course, is all level and downhill ahead.

PENINSULA

Skyline College

Distance: *400 meter track*
Hills: *Flat*
Surface: *Atlas all-weather*

There's a beautiful sign, "Joggers Welcomed," outside one of the very finest running tracks in the Bay Area, at Skyline College Stadium in San Bruno. The track is so good and the environs so pleasant that even the day or two a week of interval workouts becomes tolerable. (Well, almost!) To reach the track, take College Drive west from Skyline Boulevard (Highway 35) in San Bruno. It leads directly onto the track side of the campus. Parking lot #5 is closest. SamTrans bus routes 20J and 21B serve Skyline College, and both pass the Daly City BART station.

The track is newly resurfaced and it's super springy — a pleasure to run on. Use the grassy area and the many hurdles (even a steeplechase jump) for stretching exercises. The inner warm-up lane is of rubber and tanbark. There are nine well-marked, staggered lanes. The inner lane is 400 meters (437.44 yards) around. The track is always open to the public, due to the helpful attitude of the Skyline Athletic Department. Though there's no direct lighting, the nearby street lights serve adequately, except on foggy nights.

For more varied workouts, there are several other running possibilities available at Skyline. For one, a Parcourse passes through the stadium. Its 1½ mile route contains 18 exercise stations. The beginning is between the gym and tennis courts. You can also run, as many do, on the paved perimeter road around the campus. It's a 1⅛ mile loop with a modest 125–foot hill. The views are surprisingly good, particularly from the western vista point.

For real cross-country hill work, try running up Sweeney Ridge. That's the former Coast Guard area now open, as the sign says, ''for the use and enjoyment of the people.'' The main gravel path begins just above the east end of parking lot #2. The road is short, but it's a 275–foot climb to the top. An old white building marks the 925–foot summit. You'll see great vistas of the Bay Area. The San Francisco jail is just below to the east.

The truly adventurous can continue still further, on a very steep up-and-down trail towards the green buildings on top of the next ridge. That will lead you to a long series of cross-country trails on the Peninsula's backbone. The stone monument marking where Gaspar de Portola became, in 1769, the first European to see San Francisco Bay is ½ mile beyond those green buildings.

Hillsborough Loop

Distance: *2.2 miles*
Hills: *None*
Surface: *Asphalt*

Quite a few runners have been drawn to the unique charm of Hillsborough, one of the wealthiest communities in the Bay Area. It has a mild climate, spectacular homes and gardens, and believe it or not—no telephone poles, stores or even sidewalks. This run travels through the level northeastern section of Hillsborough, and you'll see enough of the grand mansions and views to bring you back again.

Take the Broadway-Burlingame exit west off Highway 101. Go left on El Camino Real (south) 3/4 mile, just past the Hillsborough Town Hall to Floribunda Road. Turn right and continue to the road's end at Eucalyptus Avenue. The route begins from the adjoining William H. Crocker and North Hillsborough Elementary Schools. It's one block left to the school entrance and parking area. San Mateo County Transit (SamTrans) bus 5M from San Francisco stops at Floribunda and El Camino Real.

There are bathrooms and fountains on the school grounds, along with a children's playground, tennis courts and a grassy field for stretching.

As you'll notice, the school borders the Burlingame Country Club, perhaps the most famous private golf club in the Bay Area. You might want to tour its well-manicured grounds, but running is discouraged by "No Trespassing" signs. Run southeast, away from the club, on Eucalyptus Avenue. The first intersection is

Eucalyptus Avenue (Photo by Trudi Edelman)

Ralston Avenue. Continue straight past Ralston another block, then go left at Barroilhet Avenue.

You have glimpses of some of the many private tennis courts in the area. The minimum size of a Hillsborough lot is a half-acre. Go left onto Hillsborough Boulevard, busy by local standards but sleepy by all other measures. There are no other turns for over a mile. Enjoy the lovely homes, visible without the high hedges found in other parts of the town. Cross Ralston Avenue again. The golf course appears to the left. Continue past Floribunda, where Hillsborough Boulevard becomes Sharon Avenue, the run's one-mile mark.

The driveway to a large, wooded estate branches off to the left at 813 Sharon. Just beyond, to the right, is a gateway at Manor Drive. This is the former Newhall Estate, "La Dolphine," now an elegant subdivision. The main house, modeled after Versailles' Petit Trianon, still stands. At the next intersection,

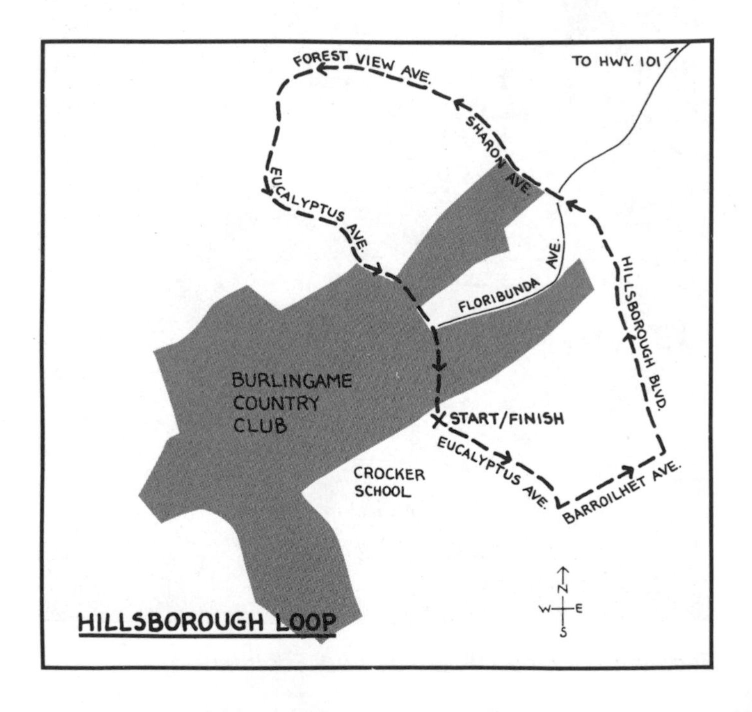

Sharon gives way to Forest View Avenue. The road bends slightly to the left and enters the shade of tall, stately Monterey pines.

Forest View meets Eucalyptus by an ornate iron gate with red brick pillars, the entrance to the cul-de-sac of Geri Lane. Follow Eucalyptus to the left. Enormous eucalyptus trees line the road as it passes through the golf course. All too soon, you spot the gates of the Burlingame Country Club and the end of the loop.

Belmont Cross-Country

Distance: *2.9, 4.1, and 6.2 miles*
Hills: *Several; rolling terrain*
Surface: *Packed dirt*

The Belmont cross-country course has acquired a national prominence since it hosted the American trials for the international Cross-Country Championships. The course has guiding signs and mileage markers for three different routes — the 2.9 miles run by high schoolers, the 4.1 miles used in junior college meets, and the 10 kilometer (6.2 miles) route used in many other races. The paths are well–maintained. While there's no shade, the ridge is generally cool enough to run, even in summer.

To reach the course from Interstate 280, take the Highway 92 exit east towards San Mateo. From Highway 92 turn off onto Ralston Ave.; from Ralston turn right on Hallmark Drive. In about one mile, look for the almost hidden entry between 2565 and 2569 Hallmark. There is a small parking area at the end of the driveway by the tennis courts. SamTrans bus route 45B from the Ralston-El Camino Real intersection in Belmont passes along Hallmark. Enter through the gate and walk uphill, past the water fountain, toward the blue bathrooms at the crest. This is the starting area for all the runs. Try to spot the tree and plaque dedicated to Bob Rush, long-time cross-country coach at the College of San Mateo. He has been largely responsible for the conception, design, and maintenance of this course on San Francisco Water Department land. One special feature of his design is the concern for spectators. From the crest, virtually the entire course is visible, and the area has accommodated 5,000 spectators at one time.

The 2.9 and 4.1 mile routes begin behind the line formed by two orange and yellow stakes with an "S" painted on them. The 6.2 mile course begins just behind that, marked by two blue stakes, also with an "S." These color codings are used throughout the course. (Although the three different routes are described here, you'll still need to refer to the map because the loops can get a bit confusing.) So pick a distance and go.

For the 2.9 mile high school course, face west and run downhill on the righthand path, in the opposite direc-

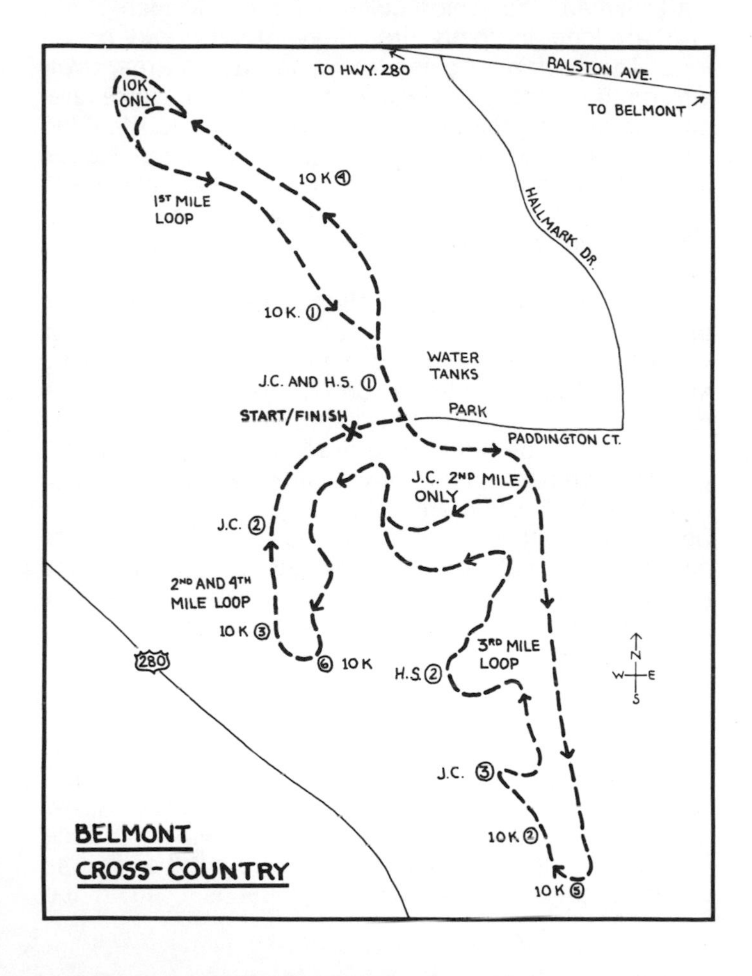

tion from the parking lot. The downhill flattens out as you approach the houses beyond the fence. (Brown signs with yellow writing will direct you.) The first turn, in one-half mile, is clearly marked. Loop back towards the start. That means an uphill, the stiffest of the course. Just before the crest is the one–mile mark.

Back at the start, continue down the left path towards the parking area. There are splendid views of the San Francisco skyline and of Mt. Diablo across the Bay. You'll pass the entrance, veering right. A sign marks where the junior college course branches off. Further along, the path turns, leaving the broad, gravel road. The course is rolling and quiet in this area, overlooking the verdant Peninsula ridge. You'll pass several mileage markers for the other courses until you spot the high school two–mile stake. Keep running, then brace for the final assault, up the second–toughest hill. You'll recognize the metal posts used to support a finish line, with the ending chute just beyond. All the courses stop here.

The 4.1 mile junior college course is identical through the first 1¼ miles. It then leaves the high school route at the clearly–marked sign just past the parking area entrance. It continues on its own inner loop, then rejoins the 2.9 mile and 10–kilometer path. First comes the junior college three–mile marker — you're not lost, you'll just be passing this way again. The two–mile stake is on the uphill less than 200 yards from the finish area. Reach the crest and continue around again toward the parking area. This time you'll skip the turnoff, sticking to the high school trail. You'll see the three–mile post again. There is no four mile marker because it's so near the finish line.

The 10–kilometer course begins in the same direction as the other two but does not take the first turn used by the shorter courses. Instead, it continues a bit beyond before looping back to the start. You'll note a sign for a 12 kilometer route, marking still another course. At the turn, you'll be near a trail that leads towards Canada Road and, in the opposite direction, to another course entrance gate. This part of the route is used in the

Cross-country racing at Belmont

annual *Belmont Steaks* race. You'll pass the one-mile mark near the beginning of the long and infamous uphill. Back at the start, continue towards the parking area. Follow the high school loop. You'll see the five-mile marker first (don't be too confused), then the blue two-mile post. Keep chugging and you'll hit three miles about 300 yards before the finishing area. Once back at the crest, repeat the exact same route for a 6.2 mile run.

Half Moon Bay

Distance: *3.9 miles*
Hills: *None, flat*
Surface: *Sand*

San Mateo County has a magnificent fifty-mile coastline. There are many beaches tucked into the ridges of the Santa Cruz mountains that reach to the ocean. One of the longest unbroken stretches begins just south of the breakwater in El Granada. You'll cover the first part of this beach — usually very easy to run on — along the crescent of Half Moon Bay.

To reach the starting point, take Highway 101 or 280 south to Highway 92. Take Highway 92 west to Half Moon Bay. Go right at Half Moon Bay, going north three miles. Park in the lot on the ocean side of the road by the breakwater. (SamTrans bus routes 1A and 1H pass here from the Daly City BART station.) There are restrooms and a not-guaranteed-to-work water fountain in the lot.

Clamber down the rocks, or take the path down, and begin running south on the beach. You can see evidence of extensive erosion. The breakwater, built in 1960 to create the only protected harbor between Santa Cruz and San Francisco, has concentrated the force of the ocean waves here, and Highway 1 itself is threatened. Soon you enter the Half Moon Bay city limits. Once a sleepy farming village called Spanishtown, the community has had extensive development in recent years. But you'll still see fields of flowers, artichokes, brussel sprouts, and, in the fall, the famous pumpkin patches.

The low cliffs on the left give way to a rocky barrier. Some lovely homes and restaurants are visible atop it.

A lone run at Half Moon Bay

The beach is noticeably freer from ocean debris. The running, during most of the year and in most tidal conditions, is excellent here. The beach is flat and broad and the sand gets packed just hard enough for smooth striding. However, during high tides in winter, the beach is narrowed considerably. At the bridge over Arroyo de en Medio, Half Moon Bay State Beach begins. You'll see a few more people, and some cars and campers atop the cliffs.

Run easily along the gentle arc of Half Moon Bay and let the surf work its magic. A good place to turn, for a 3.9 mile round trip, is the mouth of Frenchman's Creek. You can spot it in the dry season by the rich foliage on the left. In winter there will be a shallow flow, just enough to get your feet wet. For those who wish to run further — perhaps to meet someone waiting at a picnic site in the park — it's 1.1 miles to the blue administration building that marks the main entrance to the State

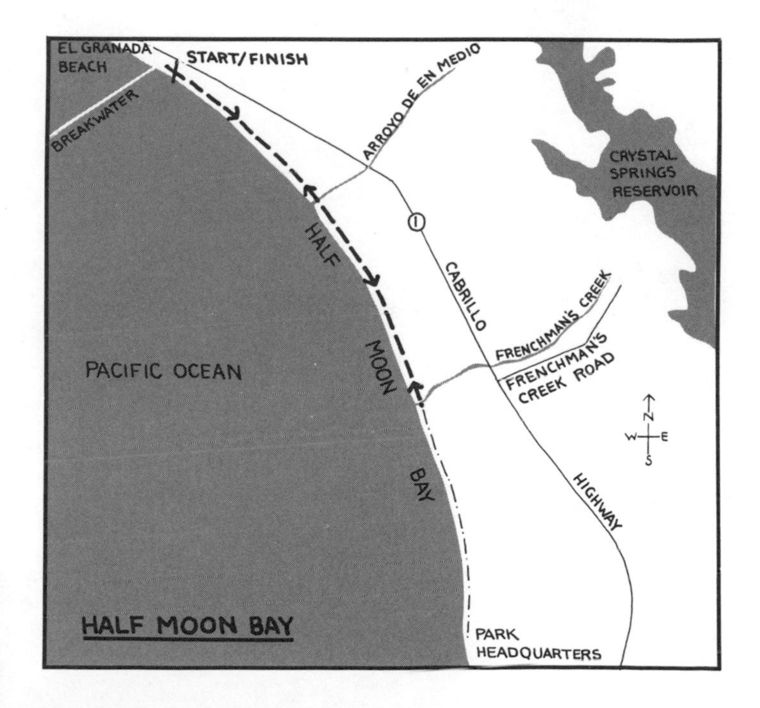

Beach. There are paths all along the way to find fountains and even showers. But the sand gets softer, and the running tougher, past the blue building. As compensation, the scenery is wilder, the huge cliffs sealing you off from all but the sound of waves.

Head back north. Pillar Point looms as an impregnable fortress battling the ocean. Above are the forested slopes of the Santa Cruz mountains. Savor the pleasures of running on a beach. Soon enough you'll spot your car.

On the return drive home, you might enjoy a visit to the James Fitzgerald Marine Reserve. It's just north of El Granada, at a well-marked sign, in Moss Beach. The Reserve offers extensive tidal pools teeming with wildlife. Unfortunately, its long beautiful beach, which extends south to Pillar Point, is just too rocky for running.

Foster City Levee

Distance: *6.2 miles (10 kilometers)*
Hills: *None, flat*
Surface: *Asphalt, dirt*

One of the most unusual places to run along the southwest shore of San Francisco Bay is the levee at Foster City. A perfectly flat ten kilometer course, which you'll follow, has been laid out on it. The course skirts the Bay, passes a wildlife preserve, and follows the Belmont Slough to within a stone's throw of Marine World-Africa USA. Don't expect any trees (there are none), but do expect good views and afternoon winds in the summer.

The course begins on the levee by a well–marked post at the foot of Swordfish Street. To reach it, take the Hillsdale-Foster City exit east off Highway 101. Follow East Hillsdale through Foster City until it turns into Beach Park Boulevard by the San Mateo-Hayward Bridge. Continue just over a mile to Swordfish. Park along the street. (SamTrans route 44C from Hillsdale and El Camino Real in San Mateo passes this starting point.) The Saturday morning fun runs held by the Foster City Joggers and Striders convene at nine a.m. at the Nathaniel Bowditch School across the street, where there are fountains and a grassy area for stretching.

Run south-southwest on the levee, away from the bridge. The first four quarter–miles are marked in yellow on the smooth blacktop surface. The going is fast here, particularly if the breeze is behind you. There are unobstructed views of the East Bay and of the towns tucked in the Peninsula hills. In less than ¾ mile, the path veers away from the Bay and enters the posted wildlife refuge area — alive with birds and other marsh denizens. As you'll see, colorful wildflowers dot the roadside.

The pavement ends after about 1½ miles, as the path becomes dirt with loose gravel. You're far from residential development here, and there are fewer bicyclists. Your only companions may be the sleek white terns diving for fish in the Belmont Slough to the left. Continue along the levee. The two–mile mark is chalked on the path. If the sign's not visible, don't worry. Running in a very wide-open area, the road shortly veers right, within sight of the Marine World complex across the slough. Perhaps you'll hear a lion roar, or a dolphin call.

Two paths enter from the left. Continue straight. You run fairly near the houses at this southern tip of Foster City. The three-mile mark is painted on one of the telephone poles to the path's left. Shortly after, with the Bayshore Freeway just across the water, the trail loops

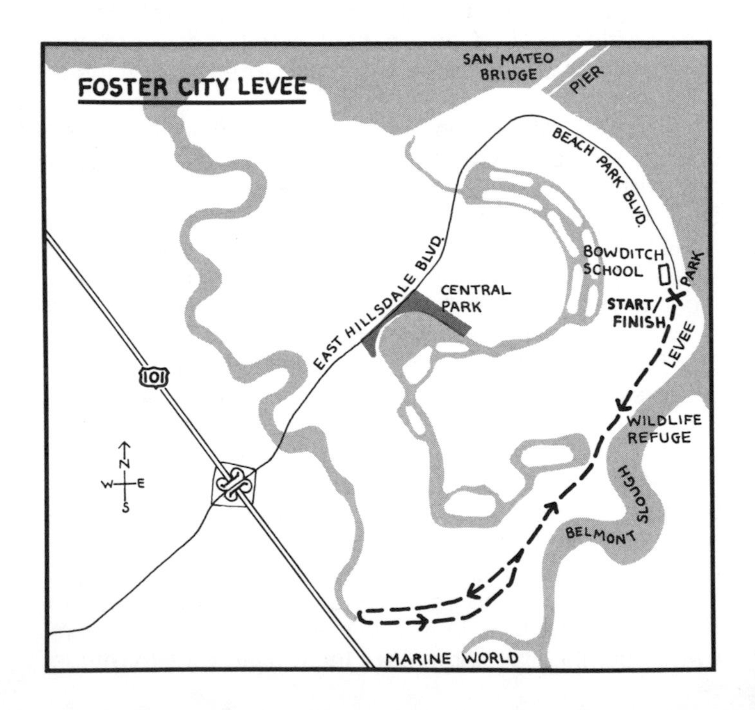

back. Four city boundaries meet here — San Mateo, Foster City, Redwood City, and Belmont.

Continue around the gravel path. Youthful motorbikers congregate in the area to the right — occasionally one whizzes by on the road. Soon the loop ends and you're back on your original route. The four-mile mark is chalked on the dirt shortly beyond. You veer left, covering familiar ground. The five-mile marker is back on the paved section. Start your kick home, and as the old Irish saying goes, may the wind always be at your back!

You can extend the run by continuing on the paved levee path. It's just under 1¼ miles to the long fishing pier in the shadow of the San Mateo Bridge. When the tide is out, you'll see people digging for clams. A good spot for a picnic after the run is Central Park, on the main Foster City lagoon. You'll see it heading back on East Hillsdale, just past Shell Boulevard.

San Bruno Mountain

Distance: *6.4 miles*
Hills: *1140-ft. gain over 3.2 miles*
Surface: *Asphalt*

For those of you who'd like to learn to run hills, try this run to the summit of San Bruno Mountain. By the way, though the Dolphin South-End Runners (DSE) lists the course at 6.2 miles, it is actually 3.2 miles each way.

The course begins in front of the Colma School on East Market and Wyandotte Avenue in Colma. The spot is at an elevation of 175 feet, so you get a bit of a headstart. To reach the start, take the Mission Street exit from Highway 280 about 1½ miles south of the San Francisco city line. At the Market Street-Mission Street (El Camino Real) intersection, it's .3 miles right on East Market to the start. SamTrans buses on route 5M from San Francisco and 5L from the Daly City BART station stop at the Market-Mission intersection.

Begin running uphill on East Market, which quickly becomes Guadalupe Canyon Parkway. Use the sidewalk at first, then the broad road shoulder. You'll see the highway mileage markers on the right side of the road — though your concern today will be elevation, not distance. Pass the Kennedy School on your left and enter the undeveloped mountain slope. The wildflowers here are plentiful in the spring. You shortly pass under a bit of shade provided by a eucalyptus grove. The cars are whizzing by; just try to ignore them.

After 1.8 miles, and a 540–ft. elevation gain, you leave most of the traffic by turning right onto Radio Road. This is the place to park for those not quite willing to do the full climb.

There's some more welcome shade from the aromatic eucalyptuses. When you leave this wooded area, the views really begin to open up. First, to the north and east, there are the highest points like Mt. Tamalpais, the Sutro Tower, and Mt. Diablo. Then the San Francisco skyline appears. Next, veering left, the vista encompasses the ocean and virtually all of San Francisco, from Lake Merced to the Bay Bridge. Continuing around, you'll see the green Peninsula. Finally, the full panorama of San Francisco Bay, from Mt. St. Helena in the north to Mt. Hamilton south of San Jose, opens up. Spectacular! And there'll almost surely be some refreshing winds to cool you off as well.

The red and white towers are your goals and they're getting nearer. Finally, you enter the tower complex, now used by only a few cable television stations since the major networks shifted to the newer Sutro Tower. At last, the summit of 1314 feet! Cruelly, the DSE (and your)

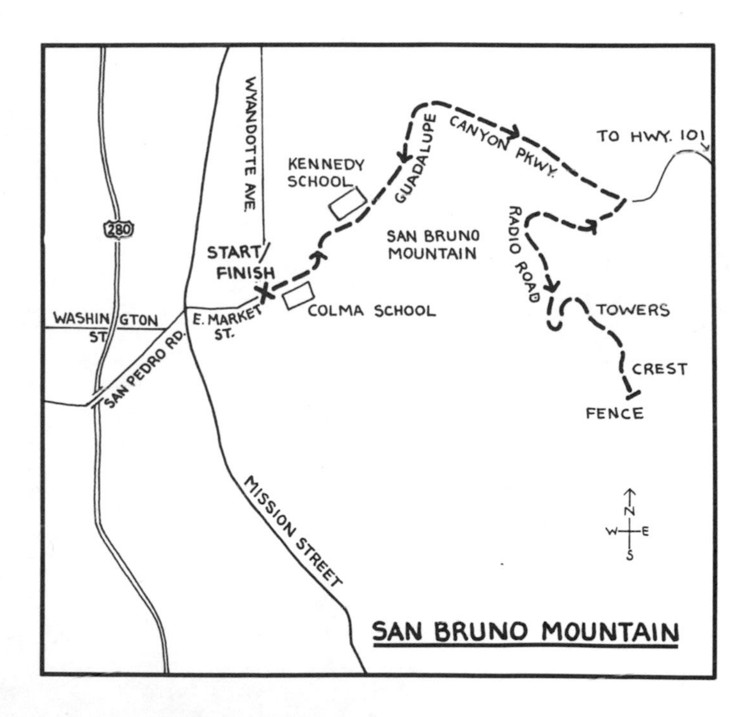

course goes a little beyond this point. It's slightly downhill to the end of the parking area. Rest and enjoy the vistas.

You'll notice that tiny upgrade as you begin back. But then comes 100 percent pure downhill. It's such a long downhill that all but the top runners should hold back a bit, or the return will prove tougher than the way up. If you have a watch, time yourself. It's roughly five kilometers from the summit to the start. Open your stride, enjoy the views, and coast to your new 5000-meter record.

Maybe you'll learn to love hills, even mountains, yet!

SAN JOSE & SOUTH BAY

Los Altos Hills

Distance: *1, 3, 4.25, 5 and 6 miles*
Hills: *Gently rolling*
Surface: *Asphalt*

Since 1973, there have been weekly fun runs in Los Altos Hills. Not a single week has been missed in that time, and the idea has spread across the country. Indeed, the Los Altos Hills runs have become so popular that the town elders tried to restrict jogging, a move that created national controversy. These Sunday fun runs are delightful, low-key affairs — no fees whatsoever, with runners of all abilities (including many beginners), certificates for all, plus a friendly bunch of people. In this chapter the several different courses used on these runs will be described. One warning, however; they're not traffic-free.

All the runs begin from Parking Lot A of Foothill College. The campus is just off Highway 280—some 30 miles south of San Francisco—in Los Altos Hills. Look for the Foothill College exit sign at the El Monte-Moody Road exit. (Santa Clara County Transit bus #52 serves the college.) As you enter the campus you'll pass the stadium with its all-weather track, ideal for warming up. There are bathrooms by the track. Fountains are at the track and just above Lot A. The weekly runs begin at 9:30 a.m. You'll note the group of people forming beforehand. (There's a published schedule of events.) First, there will be either a quarter or half-mile run in the parking area. Run to loosen up, or skip it if you wish. Everything is casual here. After everyone's finished and rested, a second run, almost always of one mile, starts. Again, it's optional.

The course is a counter-clockwise circuit of the campus on College Loop Road. After a short level stretch, you'll begin a modest uphill near the track. You'll reach the gym and run under a wooden overpass. Then it's downhill for awhile. At the bottom, on the right, is the archery area. Now climb again, past the Space Science Center, to the crest by the Observatory. It's a relaxing downhill to the finish, by the Planetarium and back to the parking lot. Someone will be calling out times. If you wish, scurry to the water fountains up to the left.

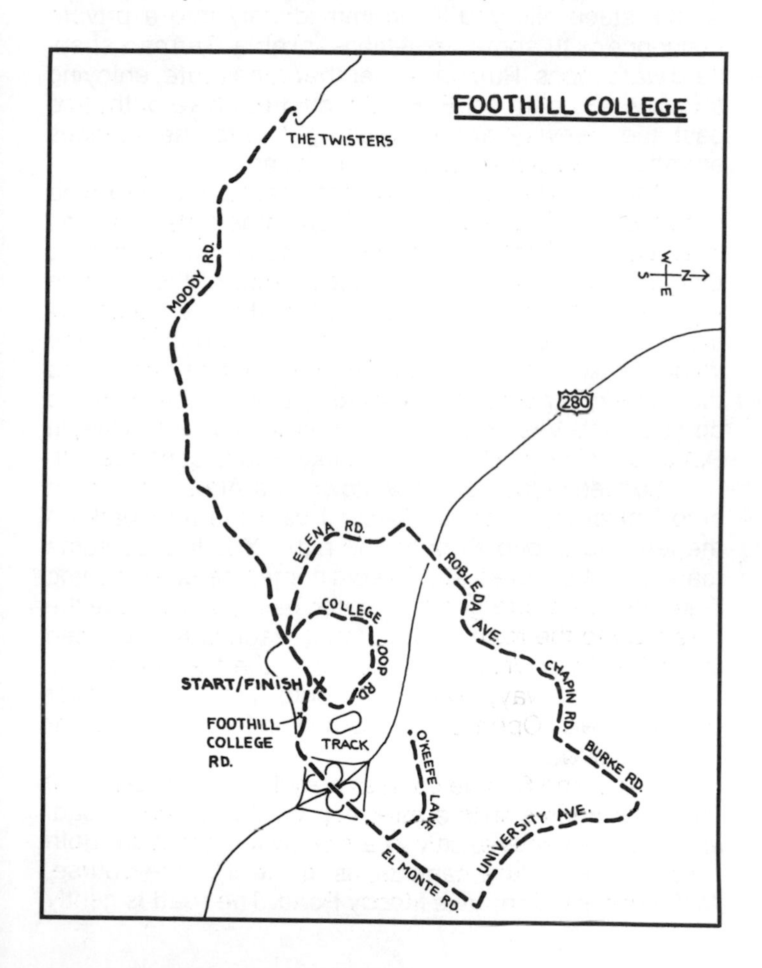

About 10 a.m., the long run of the day begins. It will be one of four distances: 3, 4¼, 5 or 6 miles. The 3–mile course heads east towards the track, then gently uphill on the exit road. You'll hit busy El Monte Boulevard. Go left, and stay on the bike path. You'll run past, unfortunately, offramps of Highway 280. Be careful. At the Los Altos Hills-Los Altos line, go left onto O'Keefe Lane. There are attractive homes at the start, then it's gently uphill past fields with horses grazing. Make your turn-around when you reach the tennis courts. If you continue up the steep hill, you'll run immediately into a private residence with some less–than–amiable German shepherd watchdogs. Run back over the same route, enjoying the view. Go right on El Monte, onto the bike path, and past the freeway again. Veer right onto the campus entrance road, sprinting to the finish line.

The 4¼ mile course leaves the campus on the road to the other side of Lot A. You'll run immediately into the intersection of Moody and Elena Roads. Go right onto Elena. It's uphill at first, with good views of the western mountains. Next is a gentle downhill, then an easy up-slope to the crest at Robleda Avenue. Go right onto the longest downhill of the run. There's a lot of shade and the scenery is pastoral — look for the old, tethered burro on your left. Veer right at the intersection with Chapin Road. Chapin quickly ends at Burke Road. Continue left.

Suddenly you're in downtown Los Altos. Turn right onto University Avenue. Follow it past the mini-park on the left and Shoup Park on the right. You'll pass some magnificent old oaks and fine old homes before reaching El Monte. It's a straight, flat stretch back, as you take the bike path to the road's right. You'll reach O'Keefe, used in the 3–mile course, then encounter the freeway again. Past the freeway, veer right onto the now–familiar campus road. Open up on the downhill to the finish at the parking lot.

The 5 and 6–mile courses are identical except that the latter begins with a mile loop on the campus road, as described above, only in a clockwise direction. Both runs then leave the campus, as in the 4¼ mile course. At the intersection, take Moody Road. The road is gently

Fun Run in the Los Altos Hills

graded, very slightly uphill. The scenery is pleasant along the way. You can see a house with a moat, the posh Adobe Creek Country Club, the Hidden Villa Horse Ranch, and the Santa Cruz Mountains to the west. Unfortunately, there are also cars, so keep to the left. After about 2¼ miles on Moody, you'll be at the turn-around point — a white house just before the "Twisters," a hairpin turn that begins a long, steep uphill. You can't miss it. Retrace your steps to the start. Enjoy the good surroundings and fellowship on the easy downhill.

After each of the runs, tell your time to the person at the desk. You then receive a certificate, color coded by the level of performance. It's a good way to keep track of your times, and to add incentive to your running. Just about everybody lingers afterwards to chat about the runs, and about running in general. You're sure to make new friends.

Fremont Older

Distance: *3.2 miles*
Hills: *One of 335 feet, another of 315 feet*
Surface: *Soft dirt*

The Fremont Older Open Space Preserve contains 466 acres of undeveloped and virtually unknown public land in the rolling hills west of Cupertino. The land was once part of a ranch owned by Fremont Older, a crusading San Francisco newspaper editor. It has been acquired, and is now managed, by the Midpeninsula Regional Open Space District. You'll find here a few well-marked trails, stunning views, peaceful oak woodland and gentle grassy slopes. There are no cars permitted within its boundaries, and you're not likely to meet another soul, even on weekends. One caution: The area can get muddy after winter rains.

To reach the Preserve, follow Highway 85 south from either Highway 101 or 280. Route 85 becomes the Saratoga-Sunnyvale Road south of the Cupertino city limits. In another 1¼ miles, turn right onto Prospect Road and follow it to its end, just past the Saratoga Country Club. Santa Clara Transit bus #96 stops at Prospect and Stelling Road. Bus route #54, on the Saratoga-Sunnyvale Road, also passes Prospect. There are no bathrooms at the Preserve. You can get water from the fountain by the golf course's 8th hole (just behind you), which has a convenient break in the fence.

Start running up the trail that leads west out of the parking lot. The path shortly forks at one of the residences that border the Preserve. Veer right into the cool, fragrant foliage along Prospect Creek. You'll pass some old stone stairways on the left. The path soon rejoins the broader equestrian trail by the only private property entirely within the Preserve. It's uphill through open fields as the vistas begin to unfold.

You'll reach a well-marked trail junction. The trail marked Stevens Creek leads to adjacent Stevens Creek County Park. You can see the trail winding up along the next ridge, where it will then descend to the park's Villa Maria picnic area. It makes a fine 5.2 mile up-and-back run, with water and bathrooms at the turnaround. Try it next time. For now, veer right and follow the Preserve's less used Loop Trail.

On the right, a sign points out the Hay Fields. (The surrounding oat stalks are cut in late spring.) Follow the trail signs gradually uphill, near an intricate power line grid. It's now a short climb to the trail's crest of 925 feet. The views, as you'll see, are extraordinary. To the north, look for landmarks like the huge hangar at Moffett Field, Stanford's Hoover Tower, the office buildings of San

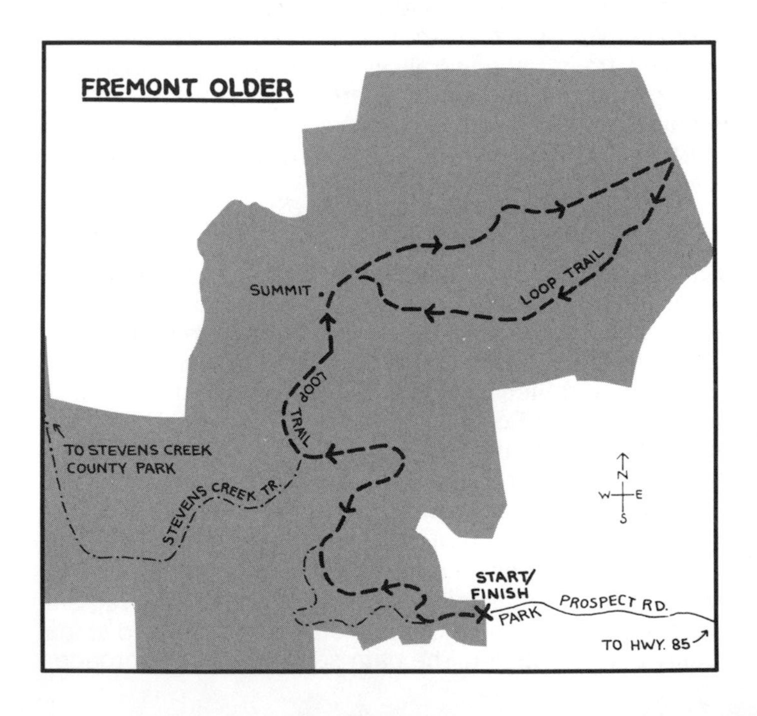

Mateo, San Bruno Mountain and the San Francisco skyline, 40 miles away. To the east is the Santa Clara Valley, still spotted with patches of green orchards despite its booming growth.

Descend on the path to the left. You'll meet a three-way junction by a fence. Go right. This short, steep downhill can get somewhat muddy. You'll pass a wooden trail post, and another marker for the Loop Trail. You return to this point when completing the loop. If there's mud on the course, go right here. (The latter two-thirds of the loop is on an old asphalt roadway. Just run down and back on it.)

The downhill trail now passes through a shady apricot orchard. You'll descend a total of 350 feet before reaching the level asphalt road alongside the creek. Veer right and run among forests of fragrant eucalyptus and English walnut trees. You might see deer, even a coyote, in this secluded part.

The path now begins its long climb. Shorten your stride, lean into the hill, and enjoy the surroundings — at least your're well-shaded. Soon you return to the end of the loop. Retrace your steps to the overlook. Then go down to the Stevens Creek trail junction, and back along Prospect Creek to the parking lot.

Coyote Creek

Distance: *3.6 miles*
Hills: *None*
Surface: *Grass, dirt*

San Jose is fortunate to have several creeks and rivers flowing through it. Along Coyote Creek, a chain of parks and open space is being developed that will include a multi-use path long enough for a marathoner in training. Here's a short part of the trail that also visits one of the hallowed sites of Bay Area running.

Take the 10th Street exit off Highway 280 in San Jose. Go one half-mile south. Highway 101 is just a mile to the east. Park on South 10th just past East Humboldt Street, by the open entrances to Spartan Stadium on the right and to a large grassy area on the left. Santa Clara County Transit bus routes #25 and #83 pass a block north on Keyes Street.

There are bathrooms for men and women, both with showers and lockers, next to San Jose State University's Spartan Stadium. Don't be intimidated by the "No Trespassing" signs placed throughout the university's athletic facilities (the main campus is a mile to the north), as the rules are bent for runners. The stadium itself is worth a visit. Many racers use its steep steps for training.

Just down South 10th, on the left, is the open gate to the university's track, Winter Field, named for the long-time track and field coach, Bud Winter. The roster of stars who have trained on this track is impressive, including Olympic gold medal winners Bruce Jenner, Mac Wilkins, Lee Evans, and Tommy Smith. Share a bit of running history and do a few warm-up laps on the track's springy all-weather surface. Then head back on the same side of the street to the entrance to the grass field. You've probably already noticed some of the elaborate exercise equipment found in the area — there are splendid stretching stations just through the gate. Try them out.

Begin running counterclockwise around the field. Just follow the fence on the well-worn path. You'll pass the track, entering the main field, used by the San Francisco 49ers for pre-season training. Continuing around, you'll see San Jose Municipal Stadium. Then to your right will be Kelley Park, your next destination. Leave the field at the gate straight ahead. (If the gate is locked, and you don't want to hop over, continue around to the next exit and run back behind the tennis courts. This will add about 1/6 mile to the run.) Go right and carefully cross Senter Road to enter Kelley Park. Run through the parking lot, veer right, and enter the park grounds by a yellow gate.

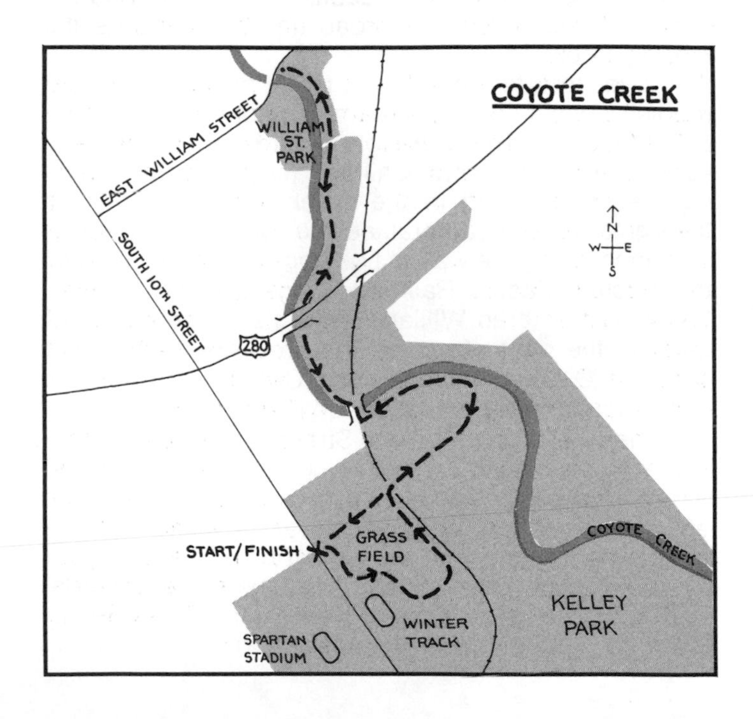

Kelley Park's 156 acres make a delightful place to visit after the run. You've already spotted the castle-like entrance to Happy Hollow Park, and the Baby Zoo, with their many attractions for youngsters. The buildings to the right house a children's theatre and the Leininger Community Center. Farther on is the lovely Japanese Friendship Garden. At the park's south end is the San Jose Historical Museum. In its eastern half are many walnut trees which replaced the Kelley family's original apricot orchard in the 1930s. Throughout are picnic and barbecue sites.

Follow the asphalt path down a slight incline past the bathrooms, then go to the left. The path ends at the back of the zoo, so continue by cutting across the meadow towards the heavy foliage marking Coyote Creek. Join the dirt trail above the creek, running north. Immediately you're beneath an overpass. Cross Coyote Creek over the two stone culverts. The water's flow is regulated upstream, so it's always fordable here. Go right up the easy bank and follow the broad trail that parallels the winding creek.

If you look to the left, you might be able to picture yourself along a country stream and not in a city of over 600,000 people. There are lots of birds in the trees and some lovely wildflowers. Children might even be catching the crabs found in the creek here. To the right, the sights are less pastoral, as you soon meet a freeway sign announcing the way to Los Angeles. Continue under the Western Pacific Railroad bridge and the freeway. You've just entered William Street Park. There are ball fields to the right. Keep on the creekside path. You'll pass the Olinder Neighborhood Center and meet the route's turnaround point at East William Street.

The other side of William Street Park is quite attractive, too. It's ringed by some of San Jose's loveliest homes. You can reach it by crossing the bridge to the left. But for this run, head back over the same route — there is no through trail on the left bank. Retrace your steps along the creek, cross over the same culverts, then back through and out of Kelley Park. Cross Senter and complete the loop of the grassy field.

Alum Rock Park

Distance: *5.7 miles*
Hills: *None*
Surface: *Dirt*

Alum Rock Park is nestled in the foothills of northeast San Jose. Since 1872, its mineral springs, believed to have medicinal qualities, have drawn people to the area. Now a more proven aid to health, running, draws many to Alum Rock. There are several hilly trails here, but along the shaded canyon carved by Penitencia Creek, there's a level out-and-back run.

To reach Alum Rock Park, take either Highway 101 or 17 south to Highway 237. Proceed east to Highway 680, then south for about 2½ miles to the Capitol Avenue exit. Follow Capitol 1½ miles south to Penitencia Creek Road. Then it's left for two miles, where you can park in the free lot at the Alum Rock boundary. There is a $1 charge for cars continuing into the park on weekends. The nearest Santa Clara County Transit bus is route #81, stopping at Penitencia and Toyon Avenue, a half-mile west of here. Fountains and bathrooms can be found along the route.

Wooden posts, well-placed throughout the course, point out the start of the Creek Trail, closed to horses. Ready? You'll run its full length. Go first up a small slope, then right at the next trail marker. The path enters the lovely, cool shade along Penitencia Creek, which flows all year. Posts with a "CT" on them are for a self-guiding Creek Trail nature walk. CT-2 marks a spot to look for wild rose, blackberries and snowberries. Other markers point out native trees, such as Fremont Cottonwood (3), Live Oak (4), Big Leaf Maple (5), White Alder (6), California

Laurel (7), California Buckeye (8), Hollyleaf Cherry (9), Willow (10), and Sycamore (12). What's at 11? You guessed it: three-leafed poison oak, so be careful.

You soon arrive at steps leading to the Richard Quincey Interpretive Stop. A train once crossed this path over the still-standing bridge supports. Although a flood washed the tracks away in 1911, most early tourists came here via the San Jose and Alum Rock Railway, built in 1891 and electrified in 1901. Continue along the barely noticeable upslope of the creek. There are good views of Eagle Rock to the left. After a picnic area, a sign directs you to cross the road to continue on the Creek Trail. This is the junction for a trail to Eagle Rock Overlook and the North Rim Trail. A popular high school cross-country course loops the North Rim Trail starting and ending at the main parking lot farther down the road. Look up and decide if you want to try it!

Continue on the Creek Trail over the bridge where the other main road into the park, Alum Rock Avenue, joins Penitencia Creek Road. Across the bridge is the Alum Rock Overlook, followed by a turnoff for the Woodland Trail, another run possibility. You will re-enter a shaded area, then meet an uphill trail leading to Inspiration Point.

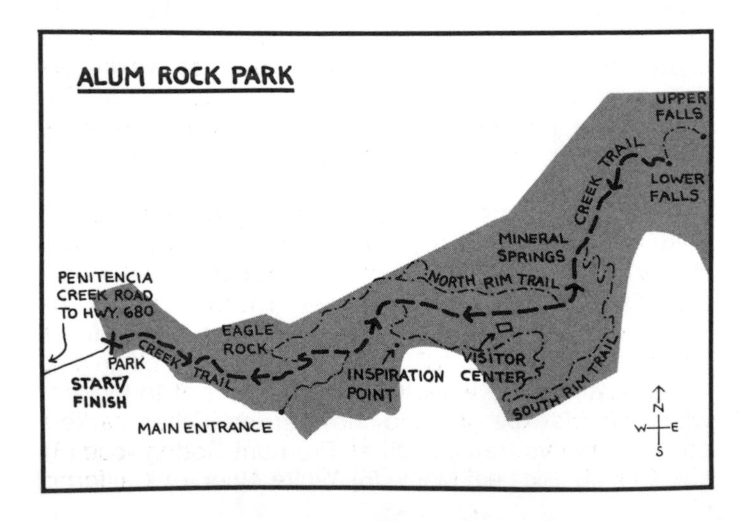

You've now entered the heart of the park. Alum Rock is rarely overcrowded — there is a limit to the hordes of visitors who, in earlier years, nearly destroyed the area's fragile habitat. Still, lots of activity will take place here on a weekend afternoon in summer. There are picnic areas, a child's playground, the ranger headquarters and visitor center, and a little further, the Youth Science Institute with its natural history displays.

Keep along the creek to the end of the main parking area. You'll notice a hint of sulphur; that's from the mineral springs. You'll see a gazebo, the park's oldest structure, with a stone fountain labeled Sulphur and Soda at its two outlets. There are many ornate drinking grottoes along the way. The mineral water is guaranteed potable in only one spot — by the MS-1 sign on the Mineral Springs Loop Trail. Take a sip.

The path becomes more peaceful again. There's a turnoff for the South Rim Trail (still another loop run possibility for your next visit to Alum Rock). The trail is serene and lovely as it crosses and recrosses Penitencia Creek. Although the footing gets a bit uncertain, you can continue safely to the creek's Lower Falls. Turn at this idyllic spot and retrace your steps — 2.85 miles back to the start. The adventurous can press on a couple of hundred yards further to the impressive Upper Falls.

Stanford University

Distance: *7.6 miles*
Hills: *One of 280 feet, one of 125 feet*
Surface: *Mostly asphalt*

There is something very special about running on the Stanford University campus. Perhaps it comes from being at one of the world's great institutions of higher learning, or from the invariably mild climate, or from the lovely architecture, or from the splendid physical setting, or from the many students and faculty who'll be running with you. The running is excellent at any time, but try it particularly in the quiet of a long, warm summer evening. This course tours the flat, main campus, then heads out onto the hills south of the university.

To reach Stanford from Highway 101, take the University Avenue exit southwest in Palo Alto. In about two miles, you'll reach El Camino Real and the pillars marking the main Stanford entrance on Palm Drive. This will be your starting point. The easiest parking is in the Stanford Shopping Center one block to the right. Santa Clara County Transit bus routes 22 and 24 stop along El Camino by the main gate and the Southern Pacific railroad station is just a few hundred feet away. Bathrooms and fountains can be found on campus.

On the path on either side of Palm Drive, begin running that broad, straight, and aptly-named road. There's a clear view ahead of the Memorial Church. The football stadium is to your left. Also to the left, off Campus Drive, is the popular running track around Angell Field. To the right, you'll see the Leland Stanford Junior Museum. Its varied collection includes the gold spike that Leland Stanford drove to join the first transcontinental railroad.

The path emerges onto the Oval. Continue straight through the Memorial Arch, dedicated to Stanford's only son, who died at age 16. You're in the Inner Quad now. The campus Visitor's Center is here. These sandstone buildings, built in 1887, are the university's oldest. Run left under colonnades, past the president's office, towards the campus' tallest landmark, the 285–foot Hoover Tower. Herbert Hoover, America's 31st president, was a member of Stanford's first graduating class.

Turn right just before the Hoover Tower onto the main campus pathway, away from cars. On the left are the undergraduate library, the book store, and the post office. To the right is the Old Union. Keep running straight

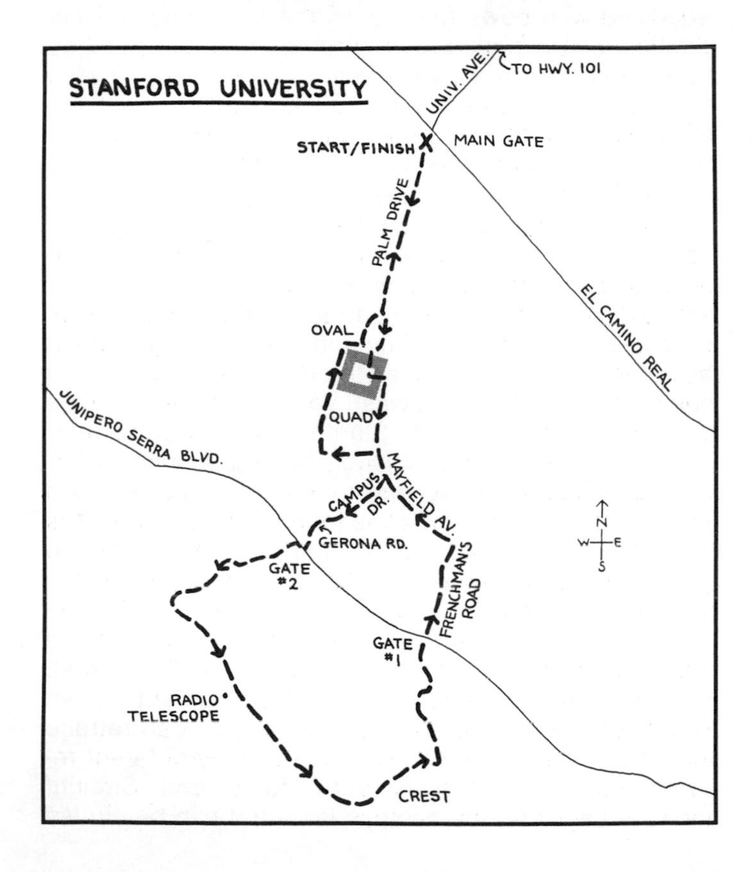

to join Mayfield Avenue. Follow it veering left, along Fraternity Row. In one block, turn right onto busy Campus Drive. You'll soon hit Gerona Road, the run's two–mile mark. Those who want to avoid hills can turn back here and retrace your steps, or freelance it, back to the start. The hardier souls can go left onto Gerona.

You will immediately notice, across Junipero Serra Boulevard, a gate with a "2" on it. Head towards it, carefully crossing the highway. Though the sign says "Private Land, Closed to Entry", you'll surely meet lots of runners. Step over the fence and run up the paved path towards the huge radio telescope that crowns the hill.

This is peaceful country, as you pass through oak woodland with cows grazing on the hill's slopes. Keep climbing on the paved road. It turns into a dirt path just as you get your first view into the valley below. There's still more uphill, but it levels off as you approach the telescope. The road is paved again at the huge disc — an eerie sight atop this hill. You've gained 280 feet in elevation in the mile from the gate.

The road descends a bit, then another uphill begins. Watch out for the cow grate. It's another 125 feet up to the highest point you reach, 525 feet. The views are splendid. To the north are the red-tiled roofs of Stanford. Beyond is San Francisco Bay and the East Bay hills. To the south and west stretches the Peninsula ridge. If you look carefully to the northwest, you'll spot the two–mile long concrete casing of the Stanford Linear Accelerator.

Enjoy the downhill. Though there are many intersecting paths, you'll recognize the main paved road back. A steeper downhill leads to the path's end. This is Gate #1. Wooden steps are provided to get over it. You're back on Junipero Serra. Directly across the road, by the white posts, is a path leading to the main campus. Enter it.

This is the run's five–mile mark. You'll pass the charming residences reserved for faculty. The street, Frenchman's Road, soon joins Mayfield. Go left. In two blocks, you're back at Campus Drive. You can retrace your steps from here, or follow the slightly different return route. Continue on Mayfield to its end. Straight ahead is Lagunita, the campus lake that can be circled

Memorial Arch at the Stanford Quad

on a dirt path. Skip that today and go right. This path leads to the other side of the main campus. You'll pass the offices of the Stanford University Press and of the *Stanford Daily* newspaper. Veer around the Earth Sciences building, past the Quad, and you'll emerge at the Oval. Run back along Palm Drive to the start.

Without hurrying,
the runner reaches his goal.

Ani, Teachings, c. 2000 B.C.

Index of Trails

PENINSULA

Skyline College . . . . 400 meters
Hillsborough Loop 2.2
Belmont Cross-Country 2.9; 4.1; 6.2
Half Moon Bay 3.9
Foster City 6.2
San Bruno Mountain 6.4

SAN JOSE/SOUTH BAY

Los Altos Hills 1, 3, 4, 5, 6
Fremont Older 3.2
Coyote Creek 3.6
Alum Rock Park 5.7
Stanford University 7.6